29/12 £2.99

D0783716

Office Politics

Office Politics

How work really works

Guy Browning

EBURY
PRESS

This book is dedicated to
Rufus Olins
whose heart is in the right place

First published in Great Britain 2006

1 3 5 7 9 10 8 6 4 2

Text © Guy Browning 2006

Guy Browning has asserted his right to be identified as the author
of this work under the Copyright, Designs and Patents Act 1988.

All rights reserved. No part of this publication may be reproduced,
stored in a retrieval system, or transmitted in any form or by any means,
electronic, mechanical, photocopying, recording or otherwise
without the prior permission of the copyright owners.

Ebury Press, an imprint of Ebury Publishing.
Random House, 20 Vauxhall Bridge Road, London SW1V 2SA

Random House Australia (Pty) Limited
20 Alfred Street, Milsons Point, Sydney, New South Wales 2061, Australia

Random House New Zealand Limited
18 Poland Road, Glenfield, Auckland 10, New Zealand

Random House (Pty) Limited
Isle of Houghton, Corner of Boundary Road and Carse O'Gowrie,
Houghton 2198, South Africa

Random House Publishers India Private Limited
301 World Trade Tower, Hotel Intercontinental Grand Complex,
Barakhamba Lane, New Delhi 110 001, India

The Random House Group Limited Reg. No. 954009

www.randomhouse.co.uk

A CIP catalogue record for this book is available from the British Library.

Cover design and interior by seagulls.net

ISBN 9780091910754 (after Jan 2007)
ISBN 0 091 91075 7

Papers used by Ebury Press are natural, recyclable
products made from wood grown in sustainable forests.

Printed and bound in Great Britain by Mackays of Chatham Plc

My thanks to...

... Andrew Goodfellow, Ken Barlow, Kate Jones, Laura Sampson and Lawrence Tejada for their cool professionalism.

Also thank you to Ralph Browning, Fiona McAnena, Malcolm Evans, Andrew Lane and Andrew Robson who smuggled out much of the information in this book.

Finally, a big thank you to my wife Esther for pointing out little mistakes that I wouldn't otherwise have noticed, such as my entire choice of career.

Guy Browning, Kingston Bagpuize 2006

Contents

Contents

Welcome to the
real world of work

Vicars and pet show organisers and other people who have very little experience of office life sometimes say they want things to be "businesslike". When you actually work in an office you know that "businesslike" tends to mean a series of escalating cock-ups relieved only by miraculous last-minute escapes and heart-stopping close shaves.

The three things that make work a nightmare on a daily basis are human error, mechanical breakdown and Acts of God. These are, of course, interrelated in that mechanical breakdown is generally the result of human error, human error is the result of Acts of God and Acts of God, on closer inspection, generally tend to be mechanical breakdown. At a deeper level there are human breakdowns, acts of machine and Errors of God, which all make for really spectacular cock-ups.

However the root cause of all office problems is the office worker. Ask one of them to do something and they will mishear, misunderstand, do the wrong thing in the wrong way and deliver it to the wrong person at the wrong time in the wrong place the wrong way up.

The one thing you can absolutely rely on at work is unreliability. That's what "businesslike" really means. If you want one hundred per cent efficiency, call in the vicars and pet show organisers. Until then, this book is about how work really works and how you can survive it relatively intact.

1

BOSSES AND HOW TO MANAGE THEM

Bosses

The difference between a boss and a High Street bank is that a bank sometimes gives you credit for things. Bosses give you things to do and then blame you for doing them. What they never understand is that if they didn't give you things to do in the first place, you wouldn't make so many spectacular foul-ups. Remind them that the less they give you to do, the less you'll mess things up.

When they're in a particularly bad mood, bosses sometimes claim they can do your job standing on their head which is why they generally give the impression of talking through their backside. And, of course, it goes without saying that no one can do their job better than them, except for their boss. This goes on all the way up the boss ladder right up to the Prime Minister where it starts again at the bottom.

Generally, bosses are older than you. If they're not, one of two things must have happened. Either you slept with someone you shouldn't have or they slept with someone you should. Or else you're very, very dim and have the career trajectory of a bus.

Bosses love to sign things. In some companies you can't pass wind before getting your boss's signature in triplicate. That doesn't mean they read everything they sign. In fact bosses don't bother reading anything except for your expenses, which they send off to a forensic laboratory for microscopic analysis.

To be fair, bosses have an awful lot of responsibility, which is why they often say "the buck stops with me". This is an American expression meaning the vast majority of the payroll stops in my wallet. Bosses also have a number of perks and the bigger the boss they are, the bigger the perk is, from company car to big company car to chauffeur-driven car, right through to "I think I'll work at home".

Naturally there are good bosses and bad bosses. Some take the trouble to get interested in what you are doing, encourage your personal development and generally provide you with a stimulating and challenging environment in which to work. There are also good bosses who lock themselves in their room, have five-hour lunches and leave you completely alone.

The board

Most executives spend their whole working life attempting to get on the board, but have no idea what to do when they finally get there. The great thing to remember about senior management in any company is that they are as surprised as you are that they're senior management. Don't be at all surprised in your first meeting to find all the directors dancing round the table singing "We're all on the board" and giggling a lot. Of course, when they're outside the boardroom, directors have to take themselves very seriously indeed otherwise no one else would.

The most tedious aspect of being on the board is that you are required to understand the figures. Although the finance director is responsible for most of this (why else would they let an accountant on the board?), you should always pretend you're totally at home with numbers. Look intensely at one part of a spreadsheet, preferably near the end, and then ask an intelligent question about it. Everyone will assume you've actually read and understood the whole thing.

In any organisation there is always a demand from the workforce to know what the board thinks and what their goals are. This can be tricky because the only goal of board members for years has been to get on the board.

Once you're there, you generally don't have a clue where to go next and you start thinking very hard about your pension pot. This is where a "listening exercise" comes in handy, where the board gathers the views of the company and then presents them back at the annual conference as the considered opinion of the board.

One of the nice things about board meetings is that coffee and biscuits are brought in at regular intervals. This is because you're all on such a high wage that the cost of making your own coffee would be the equivalent of the annual gross margin of the entire Bristol office. When the biscuits come out don't, whatever you do, select a pink wafer. This instantly marks you down as someone who would be prepared to champion an HR initiative.

People who get to the top of any organisation are generally dysfunctional human beings who are over-achieving, overcompensating or overbearing. Remember that most of your time on the board will be spent trying to manage egos the size of Denmark, with five minutes at the end of a board meeting determining the way forward for the company. You'll notice that the business that gets done in a board meeting exactly corresponds to the responsibilities of the one director who wasn't there.

The reason most people get to director level is a natural ability to delegate real work to subordinates in order to release quality brown-nosing time with their superiors. Once you have achieved the board, this delegation is formalised into sub-committees. Hard work is given to sub-committees with non-board people in them and if they work like stink they will be rewarded by "direct access to the board" and "the opportunity to influence policy" (more hard work).

Even on the board there is someone to grovel to and that is the MD or CEO. How they behave is entirely dependent on their age. If they're in their thirties they'll be preparing themselves for a bigger job elsewhere; in their forties they'll be preparing the company for sale; and in their fifties they'll be preparing themselves for retirement. Any senior management in their sixties is likely to own the company and won't be shifted on anything without the aid of a stun gun and a mechanical digger.

The chairman

At the top of every company there is a frightening, mythical beast called the chairman. They exist so far above the rest of the company that no one can actually see what they're doing. Which is lucky for them.

The chairman has to do one day's proper work per year and that is to deliver the year's report and accounts at the Annual General Meeting and speak to the shareholders or "primeval slime", as they are known in industry. The night before the AGM, the chairman will burn the midnight oil thumbing through the Bumper Book of Platitudes. Their big favourite is that "share prices can go down as well as up", an immutable financial law which doesn't seem to apply to their salary.

Chairmen all model themselves on Prince Charles. They wear beautifully tailored suits and make a point of speaking to grubby worker types so that they can keep in touch with "the people". Chairmen are also good for high-level soothing, so that when the factory burns down, spreading toxic waste over half of Europe, they can soothingly tell everyone that up until the "minor incident" the company had an excellent safety record and that there's really no need to worry because there will be an immediate independent inquiry chaired by one of their closest school friends.

Physically the role of chairman can be debilitating. Muscular control is the first thing to go and many chairmen find that they can no longer drive and have to be driven everywhere in a large car; control over their writing also goes until their signature resembles the slime trail of a dirty slug; and, most serious, they find it impossible to use any form of self-service restaurant and have to eat in restaurants where they are waited on hand, foot and gullet.

Chairmen also manage relations with the City. If you're making armfuls of cash the City likes you and if you're not the City pulls the plug on you and the workforce without a second thought. Maintaining this difficult and sensitive relationship requires a rigorous and sustained programme of lunching. A thin chairman is therefore a sure sign of a company on its way to the receivers. Chairmen are also noted for their strategic vision. After a particularly good lunch a top-flight chairman may even experience double vision.

Chairmen often give the impression that they're engaged in matters so lofty that they're simply beyond our comprehension. In fact their day is spent responding to letters that get written to the chairman of the company by little people who have a piffling problem that customer service departments simply can't be bothered with. If truth be known, chairmen are just big corporate Father Christmases helping grant little old ladies their wishes by putting a rocket under middle managers in Macclesfield.

How to impress your boss

Given the number of colossal fatheads who exist in the world at any given time, there is statistically a very good chance that your boss will also be a colossal fathead. Unless you want the inscription on your tombstone to be "He worked for a fathead", you will have to find a way of working around your boss and ignoring everything they do and say. The term for this is "upward management".

In getting round your boss, never underestimate the power of gratuitous flattery. If you can fake sincerity, you can get away with "That's a beautiful pair of grey shoes, Mr Dunne, and Velcro fasteners are so practical". Once you get into the habit of congratulating your boss on tasks that a monkey with learning difficulties could do blind-fold, you can move on to selective flattery, where they only get the big Branson/Churchill/Moses comparisons when they do something that's actually in your direct interest.

Advanced upward management is managing your boss's boss so that your own boss finds his levers of power strangely useless. There is no limit to how high you can reach with this upward management. Theoretically great upward managers could run a company from the post room. In fact it's remarkable how many apparently insignificant post-room workers claim to be doing exactly that.

Never forget that your boss has a far bigger and more important job than you have. What he wants from you more than anything else is for you not to exist except at appraisal time when he checks that you're still alive. Ideally you should do your job totally on your own without ever bothering him with problems or, even worse, opportunities.

Although your boss is far more competent and important than you, he will sometimes have difficulty with his own job. Anything you can do, therefore, to make his job easier will go down very well. The best way of doing this is to compensate for his weaknesses. For example, marketing directors don't know one end of a budget from another. Similarly, IT directors wouldn't know how to organise an office party if their life depended on it. Make these jobs your jobs.

Management is divided into managing things that are about to happen (planning) and managing things that have already happened (panicking). Bosses like to be told about things happening long before they happen. This allows them to help in the planning stage, which means putting a complete stop to it if it's a bad idea or taking the credit if it's a good idea. What's in it for you is that your backside is covered during the panicking stage when it all goes wrong because your boss was part of the planning.

Managers love it when you ask for their wisdom and experience because it assumes that a) they have experience and, b) it has given them wisdom. When they give you their experience, they will then clearly demonstrate that they know nothing and that will make you feel better.

Even when they know something, sharing it with you will mean they've lost a little bit of their edge. Keep asking them and they'll tell you all they know within the week.

Being nice to your boss is the quickest and easiest way of frightening them to death. When you invite your boss for lunch, a drink or even a quiet walk round the block they immediately think three things: he's going to resign, he's found out how rubbish a manager I am, he's going to blackmail me. When it turns out to be none of these three things, your boss will feel a profound sense of relief and have warm feelings of affection towards you. This is often a good time to ask for a rise.

Ambition

There are two types of ambition in business: one is to build a global company from scratch and become a billionaire before you're thirty; the other is to get a five per cent salary rise and a company car. The first kind of ambition is usually easier and a lot more fun because you can waste your whole life trying to get an extra five per cent from someone whose own ambition in life is to stay precisely five per cent ahead of you.

In the good old days of jobs for life, ambition was a simple matter of stepping on the head of the person beneath you to lick the shoes of the person above. Today no one in the office is ambitious because everyone is so committed to their team that they simply wouldn't take promotion even if was offered.

Ambition is a bit of a dirty word in business. To say in a meeting that you're very, very ambitious is like going on a date and saying you're very, very randy. It may be true but saying either is unlikely to get you what you want any more quickly. On the other hand, saying you're not ambitious in an interview is the equivalent of saying that, mentally, you have already taken early retirement.

Blind ambition is an interesting phenomenon. This applies to people who just want to get ahead, whether they're in word processing or fish processing. They spend

14

all their energy getting ahead but never actually know where they're going. It's only when they finally get to the top of the tree that they realise they've been barking up the wrong one.

How to get noticed

Getting ahead in business means getting noticed but working hard makes you almost invisible. It's a lot better to work hard at getting yourself noticed. One of the quickest ways of getting noticed is to be famous in your organisation for having ideas. Fortunately this doesn't mean you have to have your own ideas (if you were any good at ideas, you wouldn't be in your current job). The trick is to take credit for other people's ideas. The Japanese built their entire economy on stealing our ideas and taking the credit so there's no reason why you can't pinch a few ideas yourself and build your own career.

What senior management like more than anything else is junior management that show signs of initiative and volunteer to do things. Most of the reason for this is that the more junior management volunteer to do, the less senior management will have to do themselves. Of course, volunteering for things and doing things are two entirely different matters. Once you've got the credit for volunteering for a project, it's best to get as far away as possible from the project before the work kicks in. The best way to do that is to volunteer for another project.

Senior management are like any other layer of management in that the primary focus of their attention is upwards. They want to talk to people above them and get noticed by them. That's why it's good to get used to talking to senior management in a very informal way. Chat to them in the lift and the car park and always use their first name. They will naturally assume you are at a similar level and when your name comes up in connection with pay, promotion etc they will recognise and reward you appropriately.

Despite their soft shoes and love of pot plants, HR do, in fact, wield a large amount of power in the organisation. HR spend a lot of time loving the rest of the organisation and want nothing more than to be loved by the organisation in return. This doesn't happen because no one takes them seriously because of the soft shoe/pot plant thing. However, if you make it your personal mission to sing the praises of the entire HR department, especially in their total waste of money "Vision and Values" workshop, they'll remember you at bonus/promotion time.

The industry journal is a strange item of communication. Nobody thinks it's any good but everyone reads it. At the same time, the publishers are desperate for stuff to put in the journal. Seize the opportunity and write an opinion piece. It doesn't matter how bizarre or far-fetched the opinion is, as long as you spell it right. Make sure your photo goes in and you'll be amazed how many people see it. At the same time, everyone will be amazed you've got an opinion and begin to think of you as an opinion leader/top manager.

Everyone drinks coffee. If they don't, they shouldn't really be in business. On the other hand, no one really likes making coffee or dealing with a vending machine.

Volunteering to get someone a coffee is a quick way to power and influence. Once you know someone is a 22 or a white without, you can ask them pretty much anything in return. It's also a good way of weeding out people who are likely to be following a downward career trajectory: ie anybody who orders soup.

Appraisals

An appraisal is where you have an exchange of opinion with your boss. It's called an exchange of opinion because you go in with your opinion and leave with their opinion. Appraisals are when you get together with your team leader and agree what an outstanding member of the team you are, how much your contribution has been valued, what massive potential you have in the future and in recognition of all this would you mind having your salary slashed.

Appraisals happen once a year, usually the week after you've caused millions of pounds' worth of damage by spilling your coffee into the mainframe computer. Remember, there is no room for humour in appraisals. When you're asked, "How would you rate your interpersonal skills?" avoid saying, "What the hell has it got to do with you!" Don't forget that body language is also important. Starting your appraisal on both knees with your hands clasped in prayer may be read as lack of confidence.

In their huge amount of spare time, the HR department have dreamt up a new kind of appraisal. This they call the 360° appraisal – so called because it gives the maximum number of people the chance to stab you in the back. Some companies go in for something called self-appraisal. This doesn't mean a couple of hours in front of the mirror saying, "Tony-boy, you are the mutt's nuts." It actually means taking a long hard look at all your strengths and weaknesses and then ignoring all your weaknesses except for your "obsessive drive for perfection".

Don't forget to ask for promotion in an appraisal because if you don't ask, you don't get. It's also good to remember that if you do ask you probably won't get either. That's not altogether surprising as you are, in effect, asking for your boss's job.

When you go into an appraisal you may be thinking of how to advance your career and you can be absolutely certain that your boss is thinking along exactly the same lines, ie how to advance his career. Over the year he will have gathered together all the stringy, gristly parts of his job and will now be presenting them to you as an appetising meal. As we all know there are no problems in business, only opportunities, but the reverse is true in appraisals. If you're offered a big opportunity you know you've got a big problem.

When you've had a bad year, the appraisal is not something to look forward to. The best approach is a balance between cringing apology and grovelling sycophancy, something like: "My respect for you is so intense that it sometimes distracted me, thereby causing the continual string of major cock-ups which have been the main feature of my performance this year." Interestingly, giving appraisals is actually as hard as getting them. The secret is to mix criticism with recognition. For example: "You've made a number of mistakes, Martin, but we recognise you made them because you're a total idiot."

Promotion

Getting a promotion at work has strange physical side effects. First, it changes your eyesight so you suddenly see what a load of good-for-nothing shirkers the rest of your team are. It also lengthens your wind so that you take up ten per cent more air time in meetings. After getting a promotion most people try and prove they deserve it by becoming Business Nazi of the Year for the next three months until they run out of steam or are swiftly demoted again.

Promotion should never be confused with self-promotion. This is where you spend so much time telling everyone just how wonderful you are that eventually the company decides that it simply doesn't deserve to keep you. Also don't confuse promotion with sales promotion. This is where smiling, lizard-like wide boys promise to promote your company to the status of global megabrand by stamping your logo on a plastic key ring.

In business it takes precisely seven promotions to get to the top of any organisation. If you're promoted three times in the same year and you still have the same boss, something fishy is going on.

You know when you've had a really good promotion when you can afford to have another child. Sadly, you won't have time to conceive it until you're recovering from your stress-induced mental breakdown. Never, ever fall for the line, "We're giving you a big promotion, but your salary will remain the same." That's exactly the same as, "I really like you, but not in that way."

2

TEAMS, TEAM LEADERS AND PAs

Leadership

Leadership is enormously important in business. Everyone wants it and they're prepared to follow anyone who says they know how to do it.

In order to lead people you have to know where you're going. This destination is called 'a vision' in business or, in the real world, a mirage. When you're driving somewhere it's a lot easier to get to somewhere you've been before. It's the same in business, so you should make sure your vision is to go somewhere you've already been. This will make your job and everyone else's a lot easier. Try having a vision something like, "We passionately want to be fourth in our sector in the East Midlands."

In order to achieve your vision you need to build a team that shares your vision. Of course people don't share something unless they haven't got one themselves. So you need to pick a pack of individuals who wouldn't know a vision if one stood up in their bath. You need people who know where they're going in business and that's out of the door at five o'clock sharp. Fortunately there is no shortage of this kind of person in business and your team will be packed with them. You can then lead them anywhere until 5pm.

Baden-Powell, the founder of the Scout movement, said he would never ask someone to do something that he wouldn't do himself. It was through his courage and conviction that he led a generation of young men to wear shorts and woggles. You too can set an example for your team to follow. For example, you can show how much you trust and respect them by giving them a great deal of hard work to do. They can then follow your example by getting on with the great deal of hard work because there's no one left to pass it on to.

There's a saying in business that you can't blow an uncertain trumpet. That's why they don't let children play *The Last Post* on Remembrance Sunday. Similarly, your team won't hear your visionary message unless it's communicated clearly and effectively. The easiest and most cost-effective way of doing this is by shouting at them. You can do this on a one to one basis, perhaps even with a 360° presentation where you walk round them in a tight circle shouting. Or you can organise a conference to shout at your whole team at once. Remember to give it a theme such as "Winning Together".

Keeping your team motivated is a full-time job (which is why you have to give most of your job to them to do). People are motivated in different ways. Clearly many are motivated by money but equally there are many for whom a word of thanks will suffice to keep them working away happily for years. Make sure you pick a team of the latter sort and then employ an HR-style person to go round thanking them all the time. This will save thousands of pounds a year.

Being a leader is sometimes a lonely business. You have a lot of responsibility on your shoulders: that's why you have to wear a bespoke suit and why your team members with no responsibility have to wear safety boots. Occasionally you will have to make decisions which affect people's futures and livelihoods and families. That's when you have to show real wisdom and humility and pass the decision to your own boss.

Talking like a leader

A vital tool in being a top executive is what some people mistakenly refer to as business jargon. This is actually a specific language so that top executives can communicate effectively with other top executives quickly and efficiently, especially when they're in a train on a mobile phone.

What differentiates a business thought from a normal thought is that business thoughts have a "going forward" at the end of them. Business is all about growth and progress and expansion and you can't do that going backwards. You can alert your colleagues to the fact that you are a person making rapid progress in your career by simply saying "going forward" at the end of anything you say.

There are two things you can do with boxes in business. You can tick them or you can think outside of them. The worst possible thing in business is for you to have an unticked box inside of which you are attempting to think. No one quite knows what's inside the box but we do know that outside of the box there is a lot of blue sky for thinking in. A round box is called a silo and is equally dangerous to be in.

Executives like nothing better than going forward but this should always be done with other executives. The way to do this is to sing off the same songsheet. It's especially important to be on the same page of the songsheet and, if possible, to be speaking the same language. Often the songsheet has mood music to which it's vital to be attuned. The position to stand during the singing is onside or on board. Whilst it is good to be on board with something, this doesn't mean getting into the box.

To be a top executive you must think about money roughly twice as much as you think about sex. However, you must never mention the word money in business as this may give the impression you're not motivated by the general improvement of the human condition and concern for the environment. Instead you should concentrate on adding value and increasing margin. Efficient use of capital, investment and resources will help you increase your EBIT, yield or return and if you're lucky you might even net out on the sunny side of the street.

In the business world things are either shaping up nicely or shaping up like a pear. The latter means that the business or project is now going forward in a backwards direction. After a time progressing in a negative way, everything might go belly up or, in extreme cases, tits up. There also might be an initial cock-up which leads to the tits going up but it's best not to use these two phrases in tandem. Giving criticism in business is a matter of finding a bush and then beating round it. In order not to hurt anyone's feelings you have "friendly evaluation" which, like friendly fire, still hurts like hell.

Executives are never sacked. This would be as bad as being inside the box. Instead they are outsourced, downsized, outplaced, reassigned, promoted sideways, naturally wasted or take involuntary redundancy. Many people leave large companies because they are offered attractive packages (never accept attractive packages that you have not packed yourself or could have been tampered with).

Serving customers is not something a business does going forward. For the envelope to be pushed out of the box and through the window of opportunity, customers should first become stakeholders and then delighted beyond their expectations. In order to do this, top executives will go forward the extra mile while wearing the shoes of the customer. And remember, the customer is king (unless she is a woman). Finally, in business you can say exactly the same thing but completely alter the meaning by subtly changing the words: "When can you do a meeting?", "We must have a meeting" and "It was nice to meet you".

Arses

You may think that the most potent and popular concept at work is money. It isn't. In fact it is something much closer to home. It is the humble arse and the office is full of them.

A stupid arse is someone who chooses to do something idiotic whereas a silly arse is someone who does idiotic things because they simply don't know any better. Tight arse refers to anyone who has a fanatically clean desk, never buys a round and generally looks like they're sucking a pickled onion. A smart arse is anyone under thirty who works in IT. Pains in the arse are widespread in business. This is someone who is so often a pain in the neck that they become a permanent ache lower down the spine.

In the office there really is no legitimate excuse for arsing about. When you're arsing about and make a mistake you may well find your arse in a sling. If you go on making mistakes you may find that your arse is on the line and that your boss (or pain in the arse) gives you a serious talking to and warns you to get your arse in gear. It's important not to get arsy at this point or you may well find yourself out on your arse. Of course, if you really can't be arsed to listen to your boss having a go at you, you can always take the high-risk option and tell him to stick it up his arse.

If you want to get ahead in business you need to get off your arse or simply get your arse moving. The one exception to this is if you happen to be the rare kind of person who actually has the sun shining out of their arse. Unless you are constantly illuminating a stream of people behind you, it's usually best not to claim this for yourself. If you do, there's a real danger that people will think something equally remarkable is happening, and that you're talking through your arse.

Having an arse is not necessarily a bad thing in the business world. The trick is to know your arse from your elbow and not get the reputation for being the sort of person who wears their arse for a helmet. This avoids the embarrassment of getting things arse about face, going arse over tit and generally making a right arse of yourself. Neither should you try and be too clever in business as this in turn runs the very real danger of you being accused of disappearing up your own arse. Once you realise just how important the arse is in business, it will come as no surprise to know the overriding concern for most people in business at all levels is to make sure their arse is covered.

Teambuilding

Teambuilding events are when the managing director decides that, having spent £200 million on a new office, everyone should live outside for a bit. Teambuilding brings together a group of people who don't work well with each other in the office, takes them to somewhere muddy and puts them through a series of mental and physical exercises to prove they don't work well with each other out of the office either.

During exercises like river crossings someone will need to take charge. If you want to get across the river quickly and without getting wet, let a secretary organise it. Sadly, this is the exact time when your boss will want to prove they're the boss by organising a crossing that involves recreating conditions in the office, ie everyone standing up to their neck in freezing water while the boss flaps around on the bank attempting to make big strategic decisions. It's generally at this point when someone in sales, who already has a job offer with another company, accidentally lets slip a rope that lowers the boss head first into the water.

Paintball is a very popular outdoor activity and shows very quickly why your sales force shouldn't be allowed anywhere near your customers. Always remember to take a few little tins of paint with you so you can sit behind a tree, pour a bit of paint on yourself and pretend at the end that you've really moved the whole team spirit thing forward.

There's nothing quite so frightening as seeing your boss turn up to a teambuilding event in casual clothing. He will be wearing jeans that look as if they were standard issue in the Greek Navy in the 1950s. Even more alarming is when your boss tries to be "just one of the team" without realising that the one thing that holds the team together is relentless criticism and savage parody of the boss.

Of course all the tensions of the day will soon be forgotten in the bar where the boss will show off his ability to down a small glass of sweet sherry in six or seven sips. Suitably plastered he will then do something extremely hip like putting Led Zeppelin on the jukebox and then start snapping his fingers, which makes everybody else jump up because they think they're supposed to do something.

The lessons learned from teambuilding events are never the ones you're supposed to learn. For example, full-scale mutiny is a fantastic bonding exercise. Similarly, live ammunition does wonders for teambuilding exercises and creates almost instant supportive behaviour. Remember never to use anything you've learned outside when you get back in the office. Trust exercises would be completely inappropriate in a board meeting.

Downsizing –
teambuilding in reverse

Firing people is like being in a firing squad. Obviously it's very traumatic pulling the trigger, but not quite as traumatic as being shot. Most managers try and make the process easier for themselves by pretending it has nothing to do with them and saying things in the subjunctive like "It's been decided that you'll be going" or "Apparently, you're leaving us". It would be much more helpful if they told you the real reason you were being fired: "We're sacking you as HR director, Victor, because you hate people."

Voluntary redundancy is where you get offered a huge amount of money to sack yourself. If they had paid you that kind of money in the first place, they might have got some decent work out of you. However, it's always a nice lesson for a manager who thinks they're running the world's happiest ship to discover that every single person in their team has applied for voluntary redundancy and have been queuing since dawn to get in their application forms.

Executives complain that the two most stressful things in their work are office politics and sacking people. They could reduce stress from both if they simply combined the two: "I disagree with what you said in the meeting, Toby, so you're fired." Also, executives wouldn't find sacking people so stressful if they had a bit of fun while doing it.

They could blow up your P45 to poster size and put it in reception or throw a surprise leaving party for you with coloured "You're history, Mr Parsons" balloons.

At least sacking isn't as stressful as taking people on. When you sack someone awful they disappear, but when you take on someone awful you have to live with your mistake grinning at you across the office for years. Until you sack them.

Power and empowerment

There are two types of power in business. The first is the power to make things happen, launch new ventures and have fun. Approximately one person per company has this power and they are right at the top with the fat pay packet and wide grin. The second type of power is to say no to people and make their lives a misery. This power is widespread and it is the aim of every middle manager to have more people to say no to than can say no to him.

If you're ever in a meeting and bizarre things are happening that have nothing to do with the business in hand, there's probably a power game going on. Men like nothing better than what they call "a titanic boardroom struggle on fundamental strategy". Women have a more accurate term for this sort of behaviour – "willy waving".

Power in business is measured by how quickly you could ruin the company if you set your mind to it. Human resource departments are dedicated to doing nothing else and yet most companies seem to continue fairly happily despite their best efforts; human resources power, therefore, equals zero.

In business the power you have doesn't equate to your salary. For example, the post room can cripple a company for weeks, just for a laugh. The cash-flow problems of many companies can usually be traced to someone in the post room wedging all the incoming cheques under a desk leg to stop the desk rocking when he puts his head on it to get some sleep.

Nowadays everyone in business is empowered but some are more empowered than others. Jobs with no power feel like travelling on the top front seat of a double-decker bus. You can see where you're going but you've got no control and if you hit a low bridge you'll be the first to get it in the neck.

True empowerment is when you decide what you want to do and when you want to do it. In fact it's remarkably like being unemployed and may, in fact, be a company ruse to prepare you for imminent redundancy. In your best interests you should therefore vigorously resist being empowered at all times.

PAs

If you put all the country's chief executives in one room, all they would produce would be a range of jammy share options for themselves and some meaningless corporate waffle for the City. Give them one good PA and they might get some useful work done. That's why it's very difficult for PAs to become managers. It's not that PAs couldn't do management jobs, it's because management couldn't do management jobs without PAs.

If information is power, then PAs are the national grid of the office world. PAs are especially adept at using the phone to control people, information and power. In some cases it's because they are on the phone to their boyfriend for so long that everything else grinds to a complete halt. Good PAs, on the other hand, have the ability to shield their boss so effectively from phone calls and unwanted meetings that he or she might have died five years ago and no one would be any the wiser. Occasionally, experienced PAs lock their bosses' doors from nine to five and tell everyone they cannot be disturbed because they are in "strategic planning". Meanwhile the boss is sitting in his room wondering why the door is locked and his phone is dead.

Many of the traditional functions of the PA are dying out. For example, expertise in the boss's biscuit preference is a thing of the past. These days if a boss specifies what type of biscuit they want, the likely response from a PA is "And which orifice would you like it stuffed in?" Modern photocopiers do ninety per cent of the work secretaries used to do, collating, sorting and generally turning executive rubbish into polished documents. These positive developments leave PAs with more time to do what they do best: running the business. It's worth remembering that for every senior executive on the golf course there is a junior secretary running a major company.

Some PAs are only temps. The difference between a temp and a normal office worker is that a temp knows they're temporary. There are two kinds of temps: the first is supremely confident, gets to grips with the job in the first hour and finishes a week's work before lunch. In the afternoon she suggests a number of extremely effective ways of improving the total business and then goes home early because there's nothing in the office left to do. The first question from the second sort of temp will be, "What is that ringing noise?" You then have to explain how a phone works and only after a day's intense tuition can you move on to basic computer skills such as turning it on.

There is often a bit of rivalry in the office between PAs about their typing speeds. There is always one in every office who claims to do 120wpm. Amazingly this is always the PA who has nails that would give a sabre-toothed tiger the willies. In fact, they can type at this speed but when you read what comes out it has so many typos it looks like the first verse of the Polish national anthem. You'll also notice that PAs who claim to do over

100wpm are also the same PAs that do 10mwpd, which stands for ten minutes work per day.

PAs have many weird and wonderful abilities. One of them is being able to type lengthy documents without a single typo but not having the first idea what it's about. Another ability is that of signing letters from their boss in his absence. This can be quite worrying when you look closely at something like the Declaration of Independence and discover that many of the signatures actually read something like: Clare Howe pp George Washington.

For people who are used to word processors, it is one of the wonders of the world how PAs in the past managed to work with manual typewriters. Typing a capital P meant lifting the equivalent of 18lbs deadweight with your little finger and typing the average letter was the aerobic equivalent of an hour on the bench press.

Bosses' demands

Bosses often confuse giving dictation with being a dictator. It's a simple mistake to make and, as most bosses are fairly simple, it's a mistake they make a lot. Secretaries should be very clear that there are some things their boss should never ask them to do. Most of these are covered by Human Rights Legislation and the Geneva Convention, but there are still many demands that are legal but totally unreasonable.

For example, bosses should never ask you to arrange a meeting with more than twenty people attending. Simple to ask for, impossible to arrange. The only way to guarantee attendance at a meeting is to hold it in Barbados with all expenses paid. Even then it's unlikely that anybody will be available for the actual meeting. Similarly, when it comes to arranging travel, bosses should never ask you to get them on a flight that's already taken off.

Bosses should never ask you to make coffee two minutes after they've given you something incredibly urgent to do. If they insist on doing this on a regular basis a good way of training them out of it is to make sure you mix the two tasks by giving their vital document a large Olympic rings motif made out of coffee mug imprints. When they do give you mega urgent typing it would really be in their best interests if they didn't give it to you in handwriting that looked like a cardiograph readout.

Never make the mistake of thinking that because she's called a personal assistant she's there to assist you with personal things. You should never ask your PA to buy a present for your spouse which is thoughtful, caring and sensitive for under a tenner. If she manages to do this, don't then ask her why she hasn't bound the 500 documents you gave her two hours ago. If you give your PA "urgent things" to do eighteen times every day she will relegate your "urgent" status to her "one day over the rainbow" status. Finally you shouldn't ask a PA to do any office maintenance such as rewiring the kitchen, rearranging the carpet tiles or installing a new computer system throughout the organisation.

PAs like to go out for lunch. By lunch they mean doing a number of essential personal chores, meeting other sane human beings to let off steam and, if they've got time, buying a sandwich to eat at their desk. Lunch isn't, therefore, the time when they want to go out and do all your essential chores like putting a bet on the 3.15 at Newbury. Never give your PA something to do at 5.30pm and expect to have it done by 8.00am. Amazingly, she has a life that doesn't involve you and your bits of paper.

The one watertight way of avoiding irritating and unnecessary requests from your boss (other than feigning death) is to say that you would love to do whatever petty, pointless task they have in mind, but sadly you are currently fully employed in an even more petty and pointless task for their boss.

3

GETTING AND
LEAVING A JOB

Job search

One of the reasons so many people work in offices is because they apply for jobs that say "Executive Opportunity" when what they offer is "Series of Irritating Chores". Looking at job ads when you've already got a job is like looking at personal ads when you're already married. To put you off doing this, it's worth remembering that every job advertised has driven the last occupant to resignation or suicide.

Some people never bother to apply for advertised jobs because they think that there will be fifty or so perfectly qualified and strikingly good-looking people also applying. To put your mind at rest, simply look round your current office at the rabble of incompetent clock-watchers and remind yourself that every single one of them was the best person for the job at the interview stage. That's how rubbish the competition is.

The first thing people look at in a job ad is the salary. That's why you can advertise for a chief executive at 200K and get a pack of plumbers, carpet fitters and assistant librarians applying. The next thing they look at is the location. If it's Swindon the salary could be 500K and you'd still only get a trickle of interest from industrial archaeologists and people who were born and bred in Swindon and have developed an immunity to it. Salaries of "Up to

45K" mean that's what you'll get if you agree to take a cut from 60K. Otherwise it's 30K. Size of recruitment ad is important. A full-page colour ad in *The Economist* is likely to be more lucrative than a small box ad in your local paper that says "Earn big money fast", although to hedge your bets it's worth applying for both.

Often it's difficult to know what the job entails. Pay no attention to the job description unless it's something incredibly specific like stonemason or ship broker. Ignore anything that has words like fast-moving, marketing, executive, people-focused etc. They're all shorthand for double glazing salesman on 9K basic with commission. "All the usual benefits" means cramped office, rotting carpets, vending machine coffee, crippling workload, bastard for a boss, hormonal secretary and swingeing headcount reduction every six months. If partying and drugs are still important to you then you're probably wasting your time applying for any job with the word President in it (with the possible exception of US President).

CVs

The CV gives potential employers their first impression of you so it's vital to get it right. This doesn't mean trying to make a big impression. You need to look good, but not too good. Write your CV like you would a personal ad, buffing up your one or two good features and drawing an impenetrable veil over all the others. If you're short on achievements, simply itemise your job description, which will generally sound much better than your actual performance in it. If the people described in CVs actually existed, the business world would be packed with highly educated, multilingual, computer-literate, team-playing perfectionists instead of the knackered illiterate rabble you find in real life.

Never enclose a photo unless specifically requested to do so. People won't like the look of you unless you look absolutely gorgeous and if you look absolutely gorgeous they will assume you're thick. When you're forced to send a photo, don't raid your photo album for the one good shot of you rafting in Botswana. If you've had to try that hard, people will assume you must look pretty rough normally. The best trick is to get a passport photo done in a booth. Everyone looks rubbish in these photos and interviewers will give you the benefit of the doubt until they see you in the flesh.

Other than marriage vows, Details of Previous Salary is one of the trickiest questions you ever get asked in life. It's almost a lie detector test. If you tell them the truth, they're going to think you were pathetically underpaid for the colossal achievements outlined in your CV. If you lie, the danger is they're going to say that you're just too senior for the job. Your best strategy is to fight fire with fire and say that your previous job offered an attractive package of benefits with on-target earnings of 250K. Everyone knows this means you're on a basic of 28K with car.

Many employers still demand references even though the whole system produces more fiction than the cele- brated creative writing course at the University of East Anglia. With references you have a choice: you can get people you like to write them and have them completely ignored or get them written by your local archbishop/ football manager/Big Brother celebrity to add spice to your application. Either way they're not likely to get read because the only two appointments for which references are really studied are for babysitters and builders of patio extensions.

Most CVs can be written with the normal gross exag- geration and good old-fashioned lying, but one section needs special care – that marked "Interests". Don't put down walking or reading as everyone does that and you might as well put down breathing and farting. You should also strenuously avoid giving the impression that you have a seriously interesting life by listing glamorous things like snowboarding, quad-bike polo and nude bungee jumping. Let's face it, if you do all these sexy, happening things why would you be so interested in a career in regulatory compliance?

Your educational record should start from the beginning and work forward. But use your common sense. If you've got an MBA from Harvard it won't be necessary to include your two gold stars from Mrs Barlow for your egg-carton Stegosaurus in nursery school. CVs always ask for relevant experience. Don't be fazed by this as everyone has experience – the trick is to make it relevant. For example your time as a photocopier repairman actually had a lot of HR/IT/financial/operational experience involved in that you're bound to have worked on photocopiers in those departments.

On average every job advertised elicits about 300,000 responses. Half the battle is to avoid having your CV instantly discarded. Coloured paper is binned, fancy typefaces are binned, CVs in the shape of fish are binned, CVs with the word "psychopath" anywhere on them are binned and CVs from the person who's just been sacked from the advertised job are generally binned. The trick is to use jargon so impenetrable that people have to interview you to see whether you're actually cleverer than they are.

Headhunters

Traditional jungle headhunters work by tracking you down, shrinking your head and making you into an attractive necklace. Modern headhunters work by tracking you down, inflating your head and making you an attractive job offer.

Headhunters is a really good name for a job and sounds tough and butch. What headhunters actually do amounts to little more than business kiss-chase. However, they can be very useful as an alternative means of getting someone you don't like removed from your company. Next time a headhunter calls give them a list of the people you want to get rid of, including your boss, and see how many you can help with their "career development".

Many people in business work in the marginal, low-profile, virtually invisible sectors of IT, operations and HR. If you're one of them you must also learn the skills of sales and marketing otherwise the more successful you get in your company, the more invisible and low-profile you'll become. Marketing people move jobs more than anybody else because they spend every morning marketing the company and every afternoon marketing themselves.

Operations and IT, like the rail industry, only get attention when something crashes. For every Red Adair in the oil industry getting paid millions for putting out fires, there's a Blue Kevin, who gets sacked for accidentally start-ing the fire in the first place. Headhunters are only inter-ested in people who fix things rather than break things.

When complete losers give you their cards, it's always best to keep them. First of all you can fill your Rolodex with names and addresses and give the rest of the office the impression that you're the Schiphol Airport of inter-national connections. More important, you can pass on these names to desperate headhunters. Remember, head-hunters work out of a windy phone box in Harlow with an old Thomson Directory, so they'll be pathetically grate-ful for any help you can give them.

If you've ever wondered who reads the industry jour-nals that gather dust in reception, it's headhunters. Journals are their only way of gathering information about companies short of standing in a bush with a pair of high-powered binoculars (they do this too but as a leisure activity). Make sure that anything positive that happens in your career, even if it's getting your coffee back to your desk without slopping it, gets written up in the industry journal in the "Movers and Shakers" section.

The best time to call a headhunter is when you have a fantastic job that you're really enjoying. You're then exactly the kind of successful, thrusting person they're after. Never forget that people at the top have got there by leaving a succession of really good jobs, not by staying in them. Conversely, headhunters will not take your call when you're having a "career break". On the rare occa-sions that they do, make sure they can't hear daytime TV on in the background.

Interview technique

Most people who have a job know in their heart of hearts that a monkey could do it equally well. Of course the difficult part of any job is getting it in the first place. That's because of something called a job interview, which is a cross between a blind date and the Spanish Inquisition.

Interviews start with the knock on the door. Lesson one, therefore, is to make sure you knock on the right door. Getting all psyched up for the big entrance and then disappearing into the broom cupboard is no way to start a career in high finance.

Once inside the room, the next thing to do is to close the door, but on no account should you turn your back while doing this. If you do, the split second your back is turned is enough for the head of the panel to raise one eyebrow and for the other six members to put a large cross against your name. From then on you could have the CV of Richard Branson and still not get the job.

The next vital thing to do is to avoid sitting down. If you have watched any television at all, you'll know that really top business people take off their jackets and stand, hands clasped behind their back, staring out of the window in a visionary kind of way. So, hang your jacket on the chair and make for that window. If they don't offer you the job on the strength of that, then they're not the creative, happening company that deserve to have you.

If you must sit down try taking the chair and pulling it right up to the desk where the interviewer is sitting. They will instinctively move their own chair back and then they will be the one sitting in the lonely chair in the middle of nowhere. From this point on you're in charge. Ask them probing questions about their job and finish off with, "Thank you for coming, we'll let you know."

Contracts

Once you've passed the interview stage and been offered a job you normally have to sign a contract of employment. Contracts are the minefields of corporate life in that once you're in one you can't move a muscle without losing some vital part of your body.

The one contract that most people sign is their employment contract but strangely no one ever bothers to read it. You can't therefore complain when it's later pointed out that one of its clauses obliges you to sacrifice your first-born to the finance director. Even the innocuous clauses have little legal twists that you have to keep an eye out for: "The employee will work from 9 to 5 (or to death) at the discretion of management."

All employment contracts have three pages: page one where you start reading talks about bonuses, page three where you sign talks about holidays, and page two which you skip talks about mortgaging your soul to the company. Notice when you make a little joke about "signing your life away" the HR people laugh quickly and whip the contract away from you.

Reading the small print of your contract can tell you a lot about the company you're going to be working for – little giveaways such as "the employee, herein after called the 'worthless wage slave' ". When you're worried about whether a contract you've signed is legally binding, simply ask yourself whether you can afford to employ a team of top legal jackals to get you out of it. If you can, it isn't. A good general rule to observe when signing contracts is if the first clause forbids you to read any of the others, don't be in a rush to sign it.

Induction

Induction into a new company is very much like induction during childbirth. It's an attempt to get a new arrival quickly through a painful, messy and labour-intensive process before they realise that they were better off where they just came from.

During your first day at the office, you are generally taken around the whole company and introduced to everyone. If you remember anyone's name, they'll be the one leaving tomorrow. When you start at a new company you make friends with the first person to speak to you and then spend the next forty years trying to shake them off. At lunch-time you get taken out to lunch by a manager whose personality is exactly the same as the manager who made you leave your last company.

Induction in some progressive companies includes an introduction to the company culture. You're given a beautiful little booklet that describes how the company is creative, dynamic and, above all, people-focused, and then you're left in a dark cupboard for three hours to read it until someone else can be arsed to do something with you. Sometimes induction includes training. Mostly it doesn't and you find yourself doing something called "on-the-job training", which means finding out how to do something rather complex like reprocessing nuclear waste by a simple process of trial and error.

Occasionally you have to watch a Welcome video which contains actors in out-of-date clothing and funny haircuts talking to you as if you had just come round from an operation. You think it's just a very old video until you meet your work colleagues with the out-of-date clothing and funny haircuts.

Resignation

There are many ways of leaving your job. By far the easiest is death because it cuts out the P45, the clearing your desk and the embarrassing leaving party. Telling your boss that you're leaving the company is difficult because it tends to confirm all the bad things they've thought about you all along. Try using the language they would use if they were sacking you: "I'm afraid you're going to have to let me go" or "I'm streamlining my operation and I'm afraid this company has no part in it".

If you're the sort of person who loses your temper very quickly, whatever you do, fight against the temptation to shout, "I resign!" Bosses these days are like vultures constantly wheeling round in search of a voluntary redundancy and you'll be out of the door before you can say, "Of course, I was joking, sir." As a little reality check, throw all your money and credit cards in the bin because that's basically what'll happen if you don't keep your big mouth shut.

You certainly find out who your friends are when you resign. Generally they're the people you went to primary school with and who will still be your friends when you're in an old people's home. The people at work will think you're the bravest, coolest and most strong-minded individual to resign, in recognition of which they will avoid all eye contact and never speak to you again.

You'll know how well you've done in the company by the leaving bash they put on for you. If it's a cheeseburger at the Wimpy with Rob from accounts then you should have left years ago. If it's a champagne reception with no expense spared, you're either going to be a rich source of business in your new job or the whole company is incredibly happy that you're leaving.

Leaving gifts should really be called parting shots. When your boss says, "We've had a whip-round and we've bought you this pack of Refreshers," it's very difficult to take out a positive message about your standing in the office. On the other hand if your parting gift is a voucher at the Citizens Advice Bureau, you'd better watch out for a heavyweight breach of contract suit coming your way.

The process of clearing your desk gives you a very good indication of the reasons you are leaving. If there is nothing on your desk, you're probably leaving because you are going to a bigger and better job and you have pilfered everything from your company that can be moved physically or electronically. However, if your desk has been completely clear for the last three years of employment it may be that you are indeed surplus to company requirements. Conversely, if clearing your desk is the hardest work you've done since you joined the company, you might be leaving because there is no longer any room on your desk to store untouched work.

Alternative employment

They say that the grass is greener on the other side of the hill. Whoever they are, they're talking rubbish because, given the choice, very few people opt for the scorched brown side of the hill in the first place. So when you're sitting quietly at your computer screen in the IT department and you think that life would be much better out in the country building dry-stone walls, think again. And if when you've thought again, you still think it's a good idea, sit yourself down and give yourself a damn good talking to, because you may think it's a good idea but dry-stone wall builders up and down the country know it's a fantastically bad idea and they would give their right arm to be where you are now had they not already lost it in a horrific quarrying incident.

Building dry-stone walls would mean that you would have to be your own boss and you know better than anyone else how unmanageable you are. When you want a good gossip the options would be talking to a sheep, talking to yourself or walking fifteen miles to your neighbour who won't have anything to say anyway. Additionally, the more you work with your hands the quicker your brain turns into a mass of lard and the more you'll find yourself saying things like, "Red sky at night, my smock is alight."

The most pernicious aspect of going into alternative employment is the very real danger of being sucked into the murky twilight world of crafts. Arts and crafts are the British equivalent of voodoo and adepts develop wide-eyed compulsive behaviour by which they can't pass a piece of scrap metal, wood or cloth without lovingly hand-crafting it into an owl. Craft people continually search for craft fairs in parts of the country so remote that the locals haven't yet had the chance to laugh at their work. They then have to sit all day at their stall knitting while the bearded man at the opposite stall explains how he's rechannelled his inner energy by moving the thong of his sandals from one toe to another.

Excessive media attention is given to people who have downshifted and simplified their life. It's too good a story to mention the fact that they've actually taken early retirement on a pension five times the average wage. If your average office worker attempted to downshift, they would very rapidly find themselves living in a compost heap carving turnips into owls. And if you're going to end up doing that, you might just as well stay in IT.

4

PAY AND CONDITIONS

Money in business

If you were a fish and someone asked you what you thought about all that water, you would probably answer, "What water?" Similarly, when people in offices are asked by small children and out-of-work actors what they think about all that money the answer is likely to be, "What money?" People outside business think that those inside business are obsessed with money and spend all their time thinking about money, talking about money and tending the trees on which money grows.

People in the arts are forever talking about making money and how they don't have enough of it; at the same time, office workers are continually preoccupied with expressing themselves and doing something worthwhile which is of lasting value. That's why there are no happier people than rich artists and successful inventors. Andy Warhol said that being successful in business was the most fascinating kind of art and he should know, being respected worldwide as a successful businessman.

Saying "show me the money" in business is about as common as saying "show me your willy" and you are likely to cause less embarrassment with the latter. Sadly the real answer to show me the money is that there is no money. It's like the Holy Grail – everyone's heard of it, but no one's ever seen it. Office workers never see money;

they're paid with a slip, they shop in credit, they add value at work – and the one thing they never mention is money. Even in appraisals you can't just come out with, "I want more money"; you have to beat round all sorts of bushes like, "I feel my reward package is not reflecting the value I'm adding." Similarly, you mustn't ever tell a customer that what they're asking for will cost them money – instead what they're asking for will incur cost or, even better, will be the high-value option.

Even the people who work with money aren't allowed to admit it. There are many people out there whose jobs are money-lenders, money-takers, money-makers and money-grubbers otherwise known as bankers, financial advisers, entrepreneurs and accountants. In business the last thing you do is make money; you add value, you raise margins, you increase shareholder value, you sustain competitive advantage or you boost net profit.

Oddly enough you can only really speak about money and art in the third person: it's perfectly acceptable to say "She earns peanuts" or "That painting's rubbish" but "You earn nothing" or "Your painting's rubbish" is totally forbidden. If you're forced to pass comment face to face, the trick is to tell an artist that his paintings must be worth a lot of money and to tell the office person that they must get a great deal of job satisfaction.

Money in your pocket

They say that money can't buy you love. It used to be able to, but that's inflation for you. Money talks and what it usually says is "spend me". That's why it's impossible to hear the words "pay day" and not feel a sudden desire to go shopping. The reason why people work a five-day week and have a two-day weekend is that you can generally spend money twice as fast as you make it. In fact the less you earn the more you shop, which explains why shops are always clogged up with kids, pensioners and ne'er-do-wells. Shopping wouldn't be the same if things were labelled with the time you had to work to earn the money for them. That blouse might not look quite so irresistible if it was labelled "two days' work plus sales call to Swindon".

Companies often have mission statements stuck up on the wall explaining why they're in business. If their employees had their own mission statements on the wall, most of them would say, "I need the money." Of course if someone paid you a nice salary to lie in bed all day picking your navel then we'd all be in advertising. On pay day you can almost hear your bank account sighing with relief. Sadly your bank account doesn't know about your credit card statement.

What you get paid is shown on your pay slip. They're

called pay slips because after all the deductions your pay slips dramatically. Tax is the worst; you're taxed when you earn money, when you spend money and when you save money. The only way to avoid tax is to stand very still until you die (even then you get clobbered by death duties). And then there are National Insurance contributions, which are particularly nasty because they don't even have a no-claims bonus. Finally there are your pension contributions which give you money when you're old so that you can keep on paying taxes until you finally make it to the big tax haven in the sky.

The most closely guarded secret in the office is what everyone else earns and that's why human resource people are so smug because they all know just what you're on and give the impression that everyone else on your level is actually being paid far, far more. What really hurts is that it's probably true.

Pay

Possibly the smallest and most intense source of pleasure in the world, apart from the you-know-what, is the pay packet. Nothing is more satisfying than being given a little brown envelope full of the folding stuff, especially if the folding stuff happens to be cash. Pay packets are traditionally given out on Friday because if they gave them out on Monday no one would come to work on Tuesday.

In the old days men used to take their pay packets home, give them straight to their wives and be given a few pence back for beer. Today nothing has changed except that men now give ninety per cent of their earnings straight to the Child Support Agency leaving a few quid which is then handed straight over to the Inland Revenue.

There are many different ways of getting paid. If you have to crawl into your boss's office on your knees, beg for half an hour and your money is then thrown at your feet, you should be aware that this is not standard HR payment procedure. However, if your boss throws an enormous amount of money at your feet, feel free to do any amount of shameless grovelling.

These days computer pay slips have taken over from the pay packet and all you get is a little printout that shows you what you would have earned had it not all been deducted for tax, National Insurance, pension, mortgage and the national debt. They're called deductions because you need to be Sherlock Holmes to work out what they're all for. If you're in a hurry and you want to find out quickly how much you've actually got to spend, look for the smallest figure on the whole slip. That's yours. Don't spend it all at once.

Around about Christmas time the prospect of a bonus becomes very important, especially when you've already spent twice what you hope to be getting. Naturally, this is when you're told that this year, instead of getting a bonus, you will be put on performance-related pay. This is where they give you a pitifully insulting pay rise and if you make a performance they take it all back.

It is a golden rule in business that no one is ever paid quite what they think they're worth. If you feel this very strongly when you open your pay packet, just be grateful you're not paid what you're really worth. People at the top of the corporate ladder get something called share options. If you're not at the top of the corporate ladder there are only two things you need to know about share options: they're not for sharing and, for you, they're not an option.

Many people decide that the only way to get a raise is to change jobs. However, one of the most galling things in business is to get a job offer with a bigger salary and then to have your current company match the offer. It makes you wonder why they didn't pay that in the first place if that's what you're worth. Of course the difference is, your current employers know what you're really worth and your new ones haven't yet seen through all the rubbish on your CV.

In business everything is negotiable, including your salary. However, before you run off and start horse trading with your boss, remember that negotiation can mean things go down as well as up and that you might come out of a very invigorating three-hour negotiation with your salary, pension and self-respect all severely reduced.

Many books have been written about the art of negotiation, with titles such as *Getting to Yes*. Most ordinary people would probably be better off with one called *Getting to You Must Be Joking*. If you're ever thinking of writing a book about negotiation, don't. Anyone that reads it properly will naturally take it back to the shop and demand their money back for some completely spurious reason.

There are three basics of negotiation (but for you I can do four). First, remember that negotiation is all just a game, like rugby, for example; you go head to head with some ugly bruiser, try to get the ball and end up unconscious. Second, go in high. If they accept your first figure and you still feel cheated, it wasn't high enough. Third, you must always negotiate knowing what you want to get at the end. There's no point haggling with a cab driver to get you home if the net result is that the price is halved but you end up being dropped in Swindon. The fourth, and final, golden rule is that you've lost the negotiation if it ever gets personal. Which is why divorces are the most traumatic, agonising and expensive negotiations outside the plumbing trade.

Perks

Perks are croutons in the soup of office life; they're only burnt bits of toast but they make a very thin soup seem more of a meal. Perks are so called because when you have one they make you feel perky. If you think your job has a perk but in fact it makes you feel intensely depressed then you may be confusing a business perk with an occupational hazard. Beware of any perks that include the phrase "all you can eat", especially if you work in heavy engineering.

The top management perk is travel; a three-day, all-expenses-paid trip to see a new production facility in Thailand is to all intents and purposes a holiday and has the added spice of being done on full pay. The non-management equivalent of this is the sickie, where people decide that they worked hard enough the day before to spend a day under the duvet, out shopping and generally swanning about in their dressing gown. This, of course, has the added spice of being done on full pay. It's an interesting fact that many of these sickies tend to coincide with management trips to Thailand.

Perks vary from job to job. If you are a dustman you might pick up the odd unwanted doll which you then strap to the radiator grille of your lorry. Along similar lines, people in PR might get to bonk a minor royal and then spill the beans to *Hello!* magazine. For the millions of people who work in front of computer screens, perks are limited to computer games of sickening depravity and the chance to hack into the accounts department and adjust the decimal point on your salary.

Of course some people take perks too far: timber yard workers taking "offcuts" to construct a Swiss-style chalet in their back garden; estate agents who "house sit" a stately home for the summer; car mechanics who "road test" your Aston Martin for a week in Wales; accountants who take home a pencil for "sharpening".

Expenses

Expenses are the black economy of the white-collar world. Life itself is a legitimate business expense as long as you have the receipt. Huge creative and financial energy is dedicated to the expense claim, or "non taxable bonus" as it is also known. Doing the boss's expenses therefore is a combination of money laundering and creative accounting and any secretary interested in the possibilities of blackmail need only photocopy their boss's expense claim and threaten to send it to their spouse, the managing director, the Inland Revenue or all three.

Secretaries have their own form of expenses called petty cash, although finance directors often find it hard to see just what's so petty about £300 cash spent on "Brad Pitt calendar and other merchandise for staff welfare".

Cabbies know all about fiddling expenses and if you give them a particularly generous tip they will often give you a whole wad of receipts for you to fill out at your leisure for huge sums that would represent a taxi fare from one side of Britain to another at bank holiday rates. You can also try this trick when you're flying abroad. Get the check-in staff to give you a couple of old air tickets and claim that on your flight to Dublin you also had to fly to Mombasa for "client development".

There is a time-honoured language used to describe

what expenses supposedly cover. Anything that you can eat or drink or gives you an all-over body massage when you're by yourself is called "subsistence". Anything you eat or drink or have rubbed into you when you're with someone else is called "entertainment". And anything that you really should have bought for yourself in the shops on Saturday or done in your leisure time on Sunday is called "new business". The one thing no one has ever written against an expense claim is, "Expense probably unnecessary, please deduct from my wages."

Petty cash

Petty Cash sounds like a young country-and-western singer in a frilly denim skirt. In fact it's something of much greater value to humanity; it's a supply of cash in a tin. The definition of a small company is whether it has a small red petty cash tin. The money inside the petty cash tin is called a float because if you actually spend it all the company goes under.

Petty cash tins are full of receipts for little extraneous items. If your salary slip is one of them then your salary might be a little on the small side. Petty cash is great for last-minute purchases such as the leaving gift for Mr Martin who has worked for the company for forty years but whose leaving do has to be organised in the last forty minutes of his working life.

The key to the petty cash tin generally hangs on a string buried deep in the unexplored cleavage of Ms Panzerfaust who could rip the face off a pit bull with a light social kiss. The key is therefore as readily accessible as the Holy Grail. Ms Panzerfaust always has ten good reasons why you can't have any petty cash. When you get to reason nine, it's worth remembering that reason ten is a swift knee in the crown jewels.

Large companies don't have petty cash tins. If you spend thirteen pence you have to reclaim it through the correct channels, which means five months later you get a huge cheque for 13p signed by three directors. In big companies, petty cash becomes a cash pile, which you dip into when you need to do a bit of corporate raiding late at night after the banks close.

5

MEN AND WOMEN AT WORK

Sexual politics

These days everyone who walks erect in business accepts that there is no real difference between the sexes and that they're both absolutely equal in terms of talent, professionalism and ambition. In fact this is a myth put about by women to make men feel better about themselves, because in most areas of the office, apart from lifting heavy boxes, women have men well and truly whipped. Working women are a fact of life. Many men are still embarrassed by the facts of life. Tough.

Mothers especially have many inbuilt advantages in the office. Any woman who can run a house full of screaming children will have no trouble participating in board-level discussions; any woman who has ever warmed a bottle with one hand and changed a nappy with the other will have no difficulty working with an advertising agency; and any woman who has been in continuous labour for eight hours will have no trouble sitting through a presentation from the head of IT.

It's pretty much accepted by everybody that the workplace is becoming increasingly feminised and that the skills you need to have in business are the more feminine skills of listening, caring, compassion, empathy and great all-round communication. This will come as a bitter blow to all those women who have been carving their way to the top of organisations through sheer ability, determination and raw ambition. If this feminised workplace ever actually happens, you can fully expect most British men to be wondering around in it with a look of shock and embarrassment as if they've strayed into a lingerie department.

Men who work with women on a regular basis know that they are like visitors from another company in Eastern Europe; a lot of what they do is familiar but they do it in ways which are often puzzling. For example, women in the office bond in different ways to men, often swapping notes on dress, hair and general appearance. This is a very fine skill that takes a lifetime to acquire and men should not wade in with, "That haircut makes your shoes look bigger."

Women take things personally, which can be great because they take a human perspective and don't get overanalytical. On the other hand you have to be careful when you say something like, "the company needs downsizing" in case they go home and spend all evening on the scales.

Women are exceptionally good at listening rather than talking as they never tire of telling anyone who will listen. A woman listening sympathetically is at her most dangerous because in the space of a cup of tea and a biscuit you can reveal your secret hopes and deepest fears and then, later on, a succession of other women will listen sympathetically to the first woman passing on your secret hopes and deepest fears.

The mind of a woman is far more complex and subtle than that of a man. For example, ask a woman in the office why she's munching her way through an entire packet of ginger crunch creams and she'll tell you it's because if she doesn't finish them off, they'll just be a constant temptation to her. A man simply couldn't cope with the complexity and subtlety of this logic.

All in all, this notion of a feminised workplace is probably just another male conspiracy to create a crèche culture in the workplace to reduce competition at the sharp end. Supportive mentoring, empathy and coaching is supposed to be the feminised management style of the future. But let's face it, too much coaching, empathy and supportive listening and you won't be able to say the things vital for managing stroppy, aggressive men; ie shut up, you're wrong, I don't care, and we're doing it my way.

Male behaviour

Many women find male behaviour at work baffling at best and astonishingly brutish at worst. The answer to all this is in evolution and the fact that, mentally, we are all still best adapted to prehistory when a man's place was behind a mammoth. Many men at work still feel that their place is behind a mammoth with all the occupational hazards that entails. But in reality the modern workplace is a female place where consensus, communication and organisational skills are at a premium.

Men had only just started to walk upright when they walked into the office. Which is why you still see so much buttock-baring, chest-beating and gonad-scratching. Male chest-beating comes in the form of talking at huge length in meetings and then complaining when the meetings overrun. Buttock-baring is now restricted to manly phrases such as "going balls out on a project", or it being "cock on block time". Strangely, when things go wrong, you won't find men rushing to get the block out.

In prehistory, men didn't really need to hunt as the women grew eighty per cent of the food. Instead, men hunted to prove just how macho they were. Let's face it, if food were the issue, men would be out there hunting sheep, but how impressive would that have looked in cave paintings? In business, the activity closest to hunting is sales and that's why there is a preponderance of men doing it. They get into their cars and go out hunting for the big sales which they then report back in triumph, generally with highly inflated figures and before the ink is on the contract. Of course the national account managers are the biggest, hairiest hunters of them all, bringing back sales so colossal that the company nearly collapses under the strain of having to digest them.

Evolution isn't about survival of the fittest, it's about survival of those who can reproduce best. That is why virtually everything men do at work is some sort of sexual display. This ranges from the big Porsche-driving displays to the smaller, everyday pen-twiddling and trouser-fiddling. Shouting in meetings is exactly what stags do during the mating season and crushing other weaker males is precisely what bull walruses do on the beach.

Or another example: only men put their feet up on the desk. No one puts their feet up on the desk because it's comfortable. In reality, it's a male display thing – I can loll about like the lion king because when I choose to kill it's feast time for the whole jungle. Women have their own display thing where they go off to the bathroom and completely redesign their face with fuller lips, higher cheekbones and bigger eyes with longer eyelashes. When they get this right, they come back into the office and all the men suddenly put their feet on the desk.

Men have other bodily habits with involve the noisy expulsion of air at high pressure from both ends. Again both these habits are sexual displays in that they are supposed to communicate, "Yes, I am a big hunter, and I have feasted well on meat. Breed with me." Strangely, this and all the other male displays have the exact opposite effect on women who, in any case, are all far too busy doing eighty per cent of the useful work.

Men are happy if they have two things: confidence in their performance and toys. Men like toys because they know they can perform with them. Hence the popularity of high-performance cars with low-performance men. Men who can't perform or lose their toys tend to shout. The more they're upset, the more they shout. If shouting fails, men try the subtle approach of having a quiet drink at the pub. Sadly, alcohol tends to make men shout louder and shout complete rubbish. The best way to take the sting out of a raging ego at full blast is to say, "Sounds like you're angry about that, Ian." This acknowledges that you've heard the big jungle sound of them beating their chest and then you can get to the root of the big strategic issue that's upset them, like not remembering their birthday or whatever.

Male bores

In the office jungle the wild bore, especially the male of the species, is one of the most dangerous creatures. Learning how to deal with a male bore is a vital office skill, most particularly for women, who often seem to attract them.

Often the first you'll know that there is a male bore in the vicinity is when you find one of their buttocks perched on the edge of your desk. This is a primitive display ritual by the office bore and is closely related to the male habit of photocopying their buttocks. Male bores often lurk in lifts and have developed an ability to bore you rigid within three floors. But the favourite location of most male bores is inside your body space. This allows you to see the custard on their tie, the hair in their nose and, if you look in their eyes, the empty space at the back of their head.

Wild male bores are at their most lethal when in their own lair or office. This is where they have their small pewter cup for winning the pub quiz in 1996 and photo taken with Jimmy Tarbuck at a corporate dinner in 1989. There will also be a photo of three children who look identical to the bore except they're not completely bald. A guided tour of any one of these items can take upward of an hour. The golden rule therefore is never to cross the threshold of the bore's office. Simply pop your head round the door and give the impression that the rest of your body needs to get to an urgent meeting.

Beware of bores bearing anecdotes. When a man says, "Have I told you the one about...", say "yes" immediately. And then say, "Is it the one about the AA man jump-starting her kidney machine?" Nothing they've got is going to top that, so generally they'll fall silent and pretend they've got something else to do. Men who tell jokes generally don't have anything interesting to say. If you want to thwart a habitual joke teller, simply say you're more interested in how they feel about things. Superficial people find any kind of conversational depth very frightening, especially in the canteen.

Male bores are gregarious beasts and they like nothing better than to congregate down at the local watering hole and tell jokes. The pecking order is then established by who tells the dirtiest joke or who gets the rounds in. You are excused from getting the round in if you are providing the jokes. A woman executive trapped in this situation should immediately find somewhere to sit down and select one male bore for a one-to-one conversation about feelings. Male bores find this intimidating and will try to rejoin the pack at the first opportunity.

The worst kind of male bore is the one who is also your boss. His primary management tool will often be the golfing anecdote and any meetings with him will consist of you trying to get some sensible information out of him while he is practising his swing. The trick is to manage him better than he manages you (not difficult). Your first line should always be, "I don't want to waste your time because I know you've got a lot on" (golf). If he manages to start an anecdote, quickly say, "That's a good one, let's save it for the pub." Then avoid the pub for a week or two.

Body language

Body language in the office can be divided into two
clear messages. The first one is, "I want to get your kit
off," and this message is used by men about thirty-five
times a day, whenever there is a woman present, in every
part of the office, on any occasion from a sales meeting to
a pencil sharpening. As most men have the sexual sophis-
tication of a small dog, women are fairly safe in assuming
that any movement of any kind is a sign of male sexual
arousal. Perhaps not surprisingly, the other key message
in body language is, "Why don't you get a life, you sad
little man," which is used by women on a semi-perma-
nent basis in the office, at home and in bed.

There is one other piece of office body language you
need to watch out for which is, "You are about to be
fired." This can be an extremely subtle sign with the
slightest arching of an eyebrow indicating that your
career has just ended. Other signs can be less subtle. For
example, your boss screaming and shouting while throwing things at you and banging his own head against the
wall. It's all in the interpretation.

In the politically correct office, touching is a sexual
minefield. Squeezing past someone in the corridor can
easily be misinterpreted as attempted penetration and you
can find yourself in front of an industrial tribunal before

you can say "Good morning, Ms Mattheson". Many offices have now introduced voluntary pre-flirting agreements in which both sides waive the right to a lengthy courtroom battle before they whisper remarks to each other such as, "Can I show you my spreadsheets, Pauline?"

Rules of sexual conduct vary from office to office and country to country. For example, in Portugal, holding hands with your boss is perfectly acceptable during a sales demonstration. In America, where the rules are very tight indeed, you're not even allowed to touch a computer monitor unless it has been designated a "touch screen".

Of course all this non-touching and respecting everyone's personal space is forgotten when the whole office is forced to do ridiculous team-building exercises which involve hugging, touching and often full-blown intercourse. The only safe option is to work at home where you can sexually harass yourself to your heart's content.

Office crushes

There are two types of office crush. One is where you all crowd around the noticeboard to read an illicit photocopy of a letter from the communicable diseases unit to your boss. The other is far sweeter, and that is the crush you have on someone you fancy in the office. By crush we don't mean two sweaty bodies crushed in the stationery cupboard grasping each other's buttocks. We mean an innocent, primary school, behind-the-sheds kind of thing.

Crushes lead to odd behaviour. When the birthday card for the object of your crush is passed round and everyone else writes "Have a great day", you find yourself writing "How do I love thee, let me count the ways". The worst time is the Christmas party. It seems that as soon as you get a chance to dance with your sweetheart, the pounding disco music immediately ends and something like "Come bring me your softness" starts. You get so stirred up that you have to rush back to your desk and cool off with some tricky sales figures.

If you find yourself memorising the number of someone's favourite drink in the vending machine on the off-chance that one day you might be able to say "Of course, you're a 312, whipped with no sugar, I can tell," then you very probably have a crush on them and you're certainly a sad, sad individual.

No one ever develops a crush for anyone who works in the same part of the office because nothing cures a crush faster than seeing someone every day. It's the office equivalent of being married to someone and has the same corrosive effect on mutual attraction.

The golden rule is to never divulge who you have a crush on to anybody, ever. If you do it will get back to them quicker than a ping on their knicker elastic and from then on you won't be able to speak to them, work with them or share a lift with them. You might as well resign or ask them to marry you, whichever seems less frightening.

Office affair

If you work in an office there is a good chance that two people within twenty yards of you are regularly bonking each other's brains out. You'll know who they are because generally they're the ones without brains. Look for little tell-tale signs like continuous rhythmic grunting from the stationery cupboard, buttock prints on the boardroom table, or huge Y-fronts in someone's in-tray.

Office affairs are more common in some departments than others. In the marketing department, marketing is what you do between various positioning exercises with one of your colleagues on the top of the desk in the "innovation room". In the IT department everyone has long since forgotten how to interact with living creatures so affairs generally tend to happen with people from accounts. The HR department find it difficult to express genuine feeling and no one could possibly make love to someone who smiled all the time and called you by your first name every time they said anything to you.

There is a long and sad tradition of secretaries having affairs with their bosses. This is always a sign of a bad secretary because really good secretaries manage their boss's time so tightly that the thought of an affair wouldn't have time to enter their head let alone any other part of their body. Appraisals are often a time when hidden tensions bubble up. Key words like interpersonal, performance and flexibility take on whole new meanings and "360° appraisals" may well be the polite term for seeing your boss in the nude for the first time.

When you're having an affair be careful that your email behaviour doesn't change drastically. People having an affair check their emails fifteen times a minute and then sit with their face very close to the screen smiling inanely. Normal emails don't get this kind of response. Also be very careful what buttons you press when sending intimate emails. Get it wrong and within hours the entire global networked community will know that you like to make love in a rabbit costume.

There are three locations that all office lovers try to tick off: the lift, the aforementioned stationery cupboard and the boardroom table. It's best not to try doing it in the lift if there are only three floors in your office unless you generally have a problem sustaining lovemaking beyond twelve seconds. Don't attempt to make love on the boardroom table unless at least one of you is a director of the company or the act of lovemaking will ensure you soon become one.

Most office affairs are consummated on trips out of the office as there is nothing more romantic than a candle-lit Olympic breakfast at the Little Chef followed by a night of passion at the Travelodge. Conferences and business trips are also where most office affairs become general knowledge in the office and even someone in HR can work out that two people away for the night in one hotel room is not a legitimate team-building exercise.

Having an affair in the office heightens your erotic sense but tends to dim your common sense. That's why women coming back to the office after a long "client lunch" believe no one will notice that their neck is as red as a lobster and their skirt is tucked into their knickers. Men suddenly think it's normal to come back from lunch with wet hair and a new pair of trousers. As the affair progresses, the man's appearance will tend to change as the woman involved suggests various long-overdue improvements in his wardrobe.

There are three golden rules to follow when having an office affair: never make love within arm's reach of a staple gun; don't insist on a one-page contact report after making love; and, for women, try not to talk about "downsizing" when you first see a man naked. What betrays most office affairs in the end is that, after the bonking has been done in total silence and in utter secrecy, some people can't resist the urge to have a cigarette and you'll see them standing outside the building, with a faraway look in their eyes, puffing away stark naked.

You can tell when an office affair ends because the two people involved suddenly become incredibly businesslike and professional with each other and start behaving as if they're in an old training video. There may well be some stifled crying and rushing off to the ladies room, particularly for the woman involved. Men may start doing uncharacteristic things like going to the gym a lot or doing budgeting. In some truly disastrous affairs the two people involved decide that they really love each other and then you end up with the awful "office married couple" syndrome.

Married couples

Many people fall in love in the office. Often, for men who drive Porsches, this is with themselves. Others meet in the office, get married and become what is known as an office couple or "ring binder".

The first time you find out who the married couples are is when you spend half an hour bitching about one of the partners and then suddenly discover you're talking to the other one. But married couples in the office can be quite cute. There's nothing more entertaining than watching them try to be professional in a meeting and then one of them says, "What do you think of the proposal, darling?" The only way for them to get out of this is to call everyone else in the meeting "darling". This is OK in PR, but not in a fish canning factory.

The difference between a married couple and a couple having an affair in the office is that the married couple don't feel the need to make love in the lift (or anywhere else). What's really exciting is when you have a married couple in the office, both of whom are having an affair with other people in the office. This requires timing worthy of Swiss railways and a list of inventive excuses worthy of British railways.

One advantage of being an office couple is that you can have a drink after work and get a lift home. Just be careful you don't both turn up in the car park absolutely bladdered thinking the other one is driving. Too much of this and you become the divorced couple in the office.

Working partners

When you're young, free and single, it doesn't matter how bad a day you have at work because in the evening you can go out and drink until you forget your work, your boss and where you live. When you're older, this is replaced by going home and having a high-octane whinge to your partner.

People up and down the country must think that the offices their partners work in are an absolute technical and administrative shambles, run by cretinous bullying managers with half-baked, unworkable ideas, lackadaisically implemented by offices full of petty, egotistical shirkers. And if it weren't for their partner, no useful work would get done at all.

At home, the accepted way to respond to these work whinges is just to say at regular intervals, "That's terrible, would you like a cup of tea?" What you should absolutely not say is, "Well, if you're not happy there, get another job." Advice from partners ranges from the unhelpful to the downright dangerous. The most common advice is, "Well, you should just tell him where to stick it." This is, of course, the one thing your partner can't do, which is why they're moaning to you in the first place.

When both partners work, there are other rules to be observed. For example, when your loved one comes home from work and says, "Our new IT system is worse than the old one," the natural reaction is to say, "You're lucky you've got one that works. We've been continually upgrading for the last six years, without anything ever working." The urge to horror-trump should always be resisted. If in doubt, make tea.

Remember, however bad your day at work has been, your partner's day will always have been much worse. If you're going to make a serious claim for having had the worst day you must make sure you get home last, as your claim simply won't carry any weight if you're at home first, in front of the TV with your slippers on.

Over the course of an average year's whingeing, you absorb an enormous amount of detailed and delicate information about your partner's company. The time to make use of all this is at the Christmas party where you can casually feed back all sorts of highly speculative gossip. This makes up for the pain of having to be there in the first place. After all, this is the same company that has made your partner miserable for the last twelve months and now expects you to have dinner with your partner's boss so she can demonstrate all those personality traits that make her so loathsome to work for. If companies really wanted to show partners a good time, they would give them a Christmas bonus for all the counselling and therapy they've done throughout the year.

Maternity and paternity

Pregnancies are always good news in the office because they're proof that someone has finally decided to do something productive. It's traditional for the office to send a card to the new mother in which everyone has to write witty messages like "we always knew you had it in you".

First-time mothers occasionally bring their babies into the office and it can be quite cute having them in the office for about 3.6 seconds. For people working in the office there's nothing worse than trying to concentrate on some difficult figures and having a screaming embryo dumped on your paperwork. To get it moved on quickly, simply remark on its amazing resemblance to the chairman.

Men are now entitled to paternity leave. This is when they're allowed out of the office to see if they can find out who the father is. Men who have attended a birth are never quite the same in meetings afterwards and when you're making a crucial presentation you'll often find them grabbing your hand and shouting, "Push!"

High-powered female executives who have a baby react in different ways. Some block out time in their diary for labour, have it at their desk, pop it in their out-tray and continue with the day's meetings. Others change overnight from ball-breaking corporate juggernauts to nurturing earth mothers who spontaneously breastfeed during meetings, even when baby's safe at home with the nanny.

Sometimes juggling so many things at once can be too much to cope with. That's why there is a growing trend towards downshifting. This is a way of rebalancing your life by reducing stress at work and spending more time at home with your family. Sadly, you may find that time spent with your family is actually the cause of stress. If a survey was done at three o'clock in the morning when your screaming baby had just woken you up for the third time, the result would be ninety per cent of executives desperate to spend less time with their families and more time in the office.

6

PEOPLE AND PROBLEMS

People

Never work for a company that says people are its most important asset. If you wanted to get a mortgage and you said that your only asset was your people you would end up living in a tent. Again, beware companies that say with great sincerity that they are a people business. Roughly translated this means they are in the slave trade. If they're not in the slave trade then perhaps they mean that they are a people business to differentiate them from a baboon business. And if they don't mean that either, then perhaps what they mean is that they are in the meaningless platitude business or, as it is more often referred to, management consultancy.

It should, but doesn't, go without saying that all businesses are run by people for people. When you've knocked around for a bit, you'll know that there are really no business problems, only people problems. That's why everyone would be absolutely delighted with their job if it weren't for the people involved. In the business world people come in three categories: people who work for you, people you work for and, the most obstructive and difficult of all, customers.

The trick is to deal with people in exactly the same way as you would in normal everyday life: completely ignore them unless they get in your way or they want to give you money. Effective managers know that there is no substitute for personal contact. In a difficult and complex business situation, nothing works better than taking a person quietly to one side, listening to their issues and their concerns, sharing the learning together and then putting their genitals in a vice.

Very often people who work in offices say that all they want is to be treated like a human being. This is usually said by people who are being bullied, ignored and generally abused by the management who are all, with the possible exception of the finance director, human beings. They would be better served if, instead of asking to be treated like a human being, they asked to be treated like a can of baked beans. In this way they could guarantee that every care would be taken in their initial selection, they would be kept in a protected and temperature-controlled environment, they would be continually promoted and bring satisfaction to customers everywhere.

If you want to work for a company that really looks after you, avoid ones that talk about people. They will be as concerned with people in the same way that People's Republics are concerned with people. There is one test and one test only for a company that really values its staff: if the company does well you benefit, and if you do well, the company benefits. And you can count companies like that on two hands and a foot.

Nice happy people

Being nice in the office is like being nice on the roads – everyone likes you but you don't actually get anywhere. Nice people bring home-made oatmeal flapjacks into work and leave out a plateful for everyone to help themselves. Dig into the soil surrounding any office pot plant and you will find these flapjacks years later, refusing to decompose. Nice people also volunteer to make coffee. This is not necessarily a good thing because they cannot conceive of anybody actually liking strong coffee or tea and the only shade they make is what decorators refer to as "orchid white".

Seriously nice people answer the phone when no one else does. They then proceed to take ownership of the piffling little concern of some irritating customer and make sure something happens. Naturally they will do this while neglecting their own vital work in the health and safety department and inevitably cause a horrific meltdown that kills and maims half the workforce. Nice people are a menace.

It's very difficult to give nice people appraisals. For a start they give you a specially wrapped, takeaway parcel of home-made oatmeal flapjacks. You then have to tell them that, despite their world-famous niceness, their financial contribution to the growth of the company is zero. This is particularly difficult if they happen to be the sales director. Fortunately, the chance of niceness and sales proficiency coexisting in one human being is fantastically remote.

Nice men have the added disadvantage of having the sexual attractiveness of a tea cosy. The only chance nice men have of going out with women is when the women are recovering between absolute bastards. Nice men like to think that underneath that soft layer of niceness is an inner core of toughness. On closer examination this toughness usually turns out to be a compacted layer of niceness.

There is a small but irritatingly persistent group of people in the office who enjoy their work. They consume work like normal people consume chocolate and treat themselves to special little extra projects that involve doing more lovely work. These people have a closer physical relationship with their desks than with their partners.

Office happy people seem to have some sort of invisible stress-proof coating. Stress doesn't exist for these people because when you give them something to do with a pubic-hair-straightening deadline they smile sweetly and produce a beautifully bound report that they prepared earlier that week because it was something that really interested them. People who love their work seem to find it easier to do than normal people. They always seem to know about a button on the computer that saves five hours' work and lets them go home early with a song in their heart.

There are several explanations for the terrifying cheeriness of these people. In the media world it's a sure sign they're using a special white sweetener on their corn-flakes. In the real world it generally means an unshake-able conviction that their work is for the greater good of humanity even when it involves fitting a small rubber valve to the outlet duct of a portable sludge pump.

Occasionally, through some malicious twist of fate, these happy, smiling people lose their jobs. Naturally this doesn't make them unhappy. Three months later, when they're in a job with new-found heights of contentment, they'll tell you that losing their previous job was the best thing that could ever have happened to them.

Annoying people

Companies often say that people are their greatest asset. In reality this is only said by people like chairmen who don't actually have to deal with their greatest assets day in day out. Those who do, ie the rest of the company, know that the one thing that generally gets in the way of enjoying a job is the people who come with it.

Having a boss who is a mad axeman is obviously not good, but at least you know where you stand. What is far worse, over the course of a year or two, is someone at the next desk who sniffs. Sniffing is the world's most infuriating habit. It's impossible to like someone who is sniffing. Even the word sniffing is irritating. And it's no use offering a sniffer a handkerchief because they never blow their nose properly, they just dab at it and then keep on sniffing.

Any habit can be annoying once you've noticed it. For example, people who keep flicking back their hair with one hand and then layering it down with their fingers. These are often the very same people who spend a lot of time staring at reflections of themselves all over the office. You'll notice they position themselves in meetings where they can see themselves in the window. They also have framed pictures of themselves on their desk.

Other habits are work-related but equally annoying, like people who forward gossipy emails straight back to the person you've been gossiping about (if you're worried about this, just send your gossipy emails from somebody else's computer). Equally irritating are people who listen to all their voicemail messages on loudspeaker. A quick way of stopping this is for everyone to leave a message about how incredibly tedious it is to have to listen to his boring messages and then wait until the following day when he broadcasts them back to the whole office.

When you work with someone day in day out, you forget what a marvellous professional they are and focus on the disgusting way they handle a tea bag. Bad habits are bad for business. How can you expect to work as a team when the team leader has what looks like a hardy mountain shrub growing out of his nostrils? The only teamwork he can reasonably expect is when everyone holds him down and gives his nose a good pruning.

Some habits you can do very little about. For example, there is always one person who comes and sits next to you in the canteen. Wherever you move, whatever time you go, there they are with their tray full of cheese and yoghurt, sitting down opposite you as if you were a life-long friend. The tragic thing is, even after five years of this, you still don't know their name. Eventually you're forced to have a sandwich at your desk and pretend you're working really hard.

In general the smaller the habit the more annoying it is. When someone puts your coffee down on your mouse mat rather than your Costumes of Rural Wales coaster that you've put there specifically for the purpose, it's likely to annoy you more than larger bad habits such as persistent closing down of manufacturing plants by senior management.

Lazy people

In business these days we are all encouraged to work smarter not harder. This ignores the fact that there is a hardcore of people who don't work smart or hard, in fact they hardly work at all. They are the "motivationally challenged", traditionally known as lazy sods, and every office has at least one of them.

Strangely, lazy sods are always the busiest people in the office. Whenever you ask them to do anything there is no way they can help because they are far, far too busy. If you ever get irritated and ask them exactly what it is that they're so busy doing, they will have a long list of things that sound enormously important. The truth is, if you'd asked them the same question a year previously, the list of things would have been exactly the same.

Lazy people actually lead very full lives because they take an arse-achingly long time to do simple things like photocopying. In order to fill their days they use a special technique the exact opposite of prioritising by which they unerringly select the most trivially unimportant aspect of a job and devote their entire energy, if not their whole working life, to it. For example, they will spend three days looking for a first-class stamp to make sure your post gets delivered as soon as possible.

The only occasion lazy people show any signs of activity

are in meetings held to discuss more efficient working. Suddenly, they're bursting with all manner of schemes and innovations, all of which, sadly, they are far too busy to implement. However, they're happy to have as many meetings as you like, because to them meetings are just like being down the pub – a nice relaxing chat until it's time to go home.

If you have to work with a lazy person, you have two options. You can either ask them to do a job, remind them, re-remind them, cajole them, plead with them, threaten them, get eaten up with stress, have a nervous breakdown, see your marriage break up, drift into alcoholism and drug abuse and finally end up down and out in Swindon. Or you can do the job yourself.

You would have thought that lazy people would form an inert mass at the bottom of an organisation. On the contrary they are found at all levels in business, right up to chairman. The reason for this is simple: when something goes wrong in business it's generally because someone somewhere has tried to do something. Obviously, if you don't do anything, you can't be blamed when it goes wrong. People who sit like a lemon all day busily straightening paperclips are therefore the only people with a one hundred per cent record of success and with that sort of record, the world is your oyster.

Stress

Stress is to the modern office what the starched collar was to the Victorian office: no one likes it, it serves no useful purpose and it's a pain in the neck. But actually stress is life-affirming. It proves you're alive until it kills you and then it loses its effect, so why worry?

In fact some people love stress. Male executives like to boast about it in the lavatory, comparing how many ulcers they've got, how many marriages they've had and how long their doctors have given them to live. And then the bastards carry on working twenty-hour days until they're eighty.

On the other hand it is no longer acceptable to say your job has no stress. Admitting that your job is stress-free implies you sit there like a vegetable all day staring into space. If your job doesn't have stress it's obviously not worth doing or it's some sort of medieval peasant-type job like eel watching or stone masonry or tax collection.

The best way to avoid stress is to give stress. If you're a boss and you've got too much on your plate, just scrape it on to someone else's plate. Where's the stress in that? If you're not a boss then you can shout and scream and hold your breath till you go blue – and then come out of the stationery cupboard and go quietly back to your desk.

Many stressed business people find it a comfort to

have complex toys on their desk which have no real purpose but are good for fiddling around with, such as computers. Real executive toys that seriously reduce stress are things like a spanking new BMW 7-Series or a second home in Tuscany.

Highly stressed bosses try and pretend they're like chocolates – tough on the outside but with a soft fondant centre. If, during great stress, you've ever bitten your boss, you'll know this is true.

Upsets

Thousands of books have been written about inter-personal relationships and how to get on with your loved ones. Now that everyone is completely happy at home, someone ought to pay attention to office relationships. You will often hear people blaming political or communication difficulties when something goes wrong at work. Boiled down, all this means is that someone, somewhere has been upset.

Think how easy it is to upset someone at home and then triple it: that's how easy it is to upset someone at work. Then add the fact that you aren't linked by marriage and you haven't got that special bond that comes from having given birth to any of them (although working with some people feels as though you might have).

The quickest way to upset someone in the office is not to value their work. So when they've prepared a fifty-minute presentation, ask them to do it in five; or get together a working party on their specialist subject and don't include them; or have a team celebration and don't invite them because their job is so basic they don't really count; or ask them to do something and then tell them how to do it in minute detail; or ask them for some extra work and then don't use it; or ask them why their job hasn't been done away with yet.

Upsetting your boss is the easiest thing to do in the office (apart from their job, that is). All you have to do is turn up and you've got yourself well and truly in their bad books. Keeping on the right side of them is simply a matter of anticipating their every whim, completing work before they decide it's needed and laughing at their pathetic jokes rather than their pathetic dress sense.

The lower you go down the office hierarchy, the easier it is to upset people. If your job is to push a button you're not going to take kindly to anyone who tells you where, when and how to push it. Only those people who respect your absolute mastery of button pushing or form filling or barrier lifting will be allowed to benefit from a display of the aforesaid mastery.

The most efficient way to get something done in the office is to have said thank you to everybody the last time. If you're the sort of person who dumps on people at the last moment, screams for results and then doesn't give a word of thanks, you'll find it gets increasingly difficult to get anything done, because everyone will glue your stuff to the bottom of their in-tray.

The only sure-fire way of never upsetting anyone is to follow this tried-and-tested formula: ask someone's advice on their particular job, remember their name, listen and then thank them sincerely. When you ask them to do something, they should be most helpful. If they're not, then get really, really upset.

Personal crises

The best form of entertainment in the office is the personal crisis. This is where someone loses their temper or breaks down or tells a valued business customer they can stick their business where the sun never shines. Everyone has these crises. For some it's simmering resentment for thirty years followed by a sudden outbreak of eczema. For others, mostly men, it takes the form of very loud shouting, swearing and storming about the office. Actual physical fights are rare and tend to be between sales people who have forgotten the finer points of negotiation.

During one of these male outbursts, you should strenuously resist the urge to titter. Men who are shouting are expressing all the classic symptoms of insecurity, lack of confidence and possible deficiency in the underpant department. If they see anyone tittering they will move rapidly into the "you're fired" phase, followed twenty-four hours later by the bunches of flowers phase and a month later by the sideways promotion phase. It has to be said that not all men are like this. A violent outburst from an HR director is as likely as a burst of wit from a finance director.

Female crises in the office tend to take the form of tears and sobbing. When a woman breaks down in tears, every other woman for fifty miles joins in the handkerchief waving and general clearing up. This is due to deep instinctive feelings of sisterly support and, more importantly, a burning desire to get all the dirt and gossip first hand. One of the calming things women say to each other in moments of crises is, "He's not worth it." This probably refers to a deeply held conviction that the male in question does not have the professional accomplishments to justify his large salary.

However distraught they are, women will always grab their handbag before running to the loo in tears. Similarly, men grab their wallets before they rush out of the office to the pub, their favoured place for colleague consultation. The number of times men have to do this shows just how sensitive they are underneath.

Depression

There are two kinds of depression in business. The first devastates great swathes of industry across the globe, hastens the rise of extreme nationalism and tips nations into world war. The other is the tendency to burst into tears every time a piece of paper lands on your desk. The latter hurts a lot more on your average Tuesday afternoon.

The quickest way to feel better is to eat chocolate and then, with the instant energy this gives you, go clothes shopping. One thing that doesn't work is something called "snapping out of it". If you could snap in and out of things you'd be a multi-purpose wrench, not a human being. On the other hand, it's not acceptable to go into a meeting and say, "I'm afraid I've lost a million-pound contract but don't shout at me because I'm feeling a little bit glum."

In an office you don't have to have a reason for feeling down in the dumps. In fact you're less likely to feel blue when everything's going to hell in a handcart. It's when everything's going smoothly and you realise you're smoothly going nowhere that glumness strikes. And it's always precisely at this stage that someone pops up and tells you they've won the lottery. Your only sensible option then is to put your head in a big Jiffy bag and have a good blub. Just be careful that your head doesn't get posted to Swindon, because then you really will feel bad.

Sickies

Given the number of people off sick at any one time, it's not surprising that the National Health Service is in crisis. In reality, the closest that most people off sick get to the NHS is when they drive past a hospital on their way to the shops. That's because people aren't going to take a sickie unless they're well enough to enjoy it.

You can take a maximum of three days off with a sickie before you are required to have a doctor's note, which these days you have to pay for. You would have thought that for a couple of extra quid you could get yourself excused for a couple of months with some seriously nasty tropical stomach bug that tends to flare up around the time of major events in the racing calendar.

Illnesses that occur during a working day have a range of symptoms which tend to peak in number and intensity around about 8.30 in the morning and then rapidly dwindle to a light, generalised nausea by 9.30, for which the only cure is a rigorous bout of shopping. Of course the best sickie of all is maternity leave as you get months and months off. The only disadvantage is that, in order to make it look convincing, you have to bring up a family for the next twenty years.

If you have to phone in to let the office know you're sick, it's very important that you sound like you have pulled the tubes out of your nose and the oxygen mask off your face just to speak to them for a second before you collapse back into a coma. This can be done in a number of ways, the quickest and most effective being to put cotton wool up both nostrils and then to speak through your face flannel. On no account phone in sick from your mobile phone while driving on the motorway with *Walking On Sunshine* playing on the CD.

Treats

Working life would be absolutely intolerable were it not for the little treats we allow ourselves in an effort to dilute the horror of being empowered, working in teams and satisfying customers.

Careful time management can give rise to all sorts of treats. For example, if you arrange to go to an outside meeting at 10.45 you can get out of bed at nine. Similarly, if you're out on the road a lot you can arrange two meetings, one mid morning and the other late afternoon, and allow a huge safety margin between the two. You can then join the surprisingly large proportion of Britain's workforce parked in country lanes with your flask of coffee, newspaper and mobile phone safely switched off.

If you're stuck in the office there are different treats available. You can arrange a meeting with your best friend, work for five minutes and then have an epic gossip about everyone and everything for the rest of the hour while munching through a plate of biscuits. If you're stuck at your computer you can still exchange incredibly lurid emails about your boss even when they're sitting right in front of you. If you've got no one to email, you can just sit at your desk, put your brain in neutral and spend the afternoon rearranging your files or finding out what all those little buttons on the toolbar do.

Men and women have different treats. For men the big one is to take a pile of magazines into the lavatory and sit there happily for three hours (some men treat themselves like this every morning of their working life). Women often treat themselves by going to the shops at lunch-time and buying something completely unnecessary. This has the double benefit of having a nice big bag snuggling under your desk the whole afternoon and also something for you to take back to the shops the following day.

Some people treat themselves in ways so subtle you would hardly notice; for example, using a Post-It note or not answering a call or having their coffee whipped instead of normal or just walking up and down corridors all day holding important papers but actually just enjoying the exercise. Other treats verge on the bizarre, like simulating a personal crisis and having a long chat with HR in order to get at their emergency supply of sympathy Chocolate HobNobs.

When you deserve mega-treating, it's perfectly possible to go into work and still have a complete day off. It's amazing how one chatty coffee break can merge effortlessly into a social phone call, a long lunch, an unnecessary meeting and an early departure. There's really no greater treat than being in the office, watching other people work and knowing that you're being paid good money for doing absolutely nothing.

7

PENS AND
PAPER

Stationery

Stationery cupboards are the sweet shops of office life, a colourful pick-and-mix of lots of nice little things that you don't really need but you take a handful anyway. Hottest items in the stationery cupboard are highlighter pens. These highlight the useful and important parts of documents and prove that ninety-five per cent of most documents are neither. "Things to do" pads go like hot cakes because they give the impression that you're doing things. Stationery is, in fact, a work substitute and you'll notice that the first three things you write on your "Things to do" pad are: 1. Highlight documents. 2. Punch holes in documents. 3. Staple documents.

Biros are like Japanese cars: they're cheap, they start first time and they come in many colours. Of course Japanese cars don't have the little unexplained hole in the side. To the highly stressed executive, a biro is a complete meal. First you bend back the clip bit from the top and then bite it off. Then you mangle the top between your teeth, suck out the little stopper from the top of the pen, and crunch away at the pen itself. A standard biro counts towards one of your five portions of fruit and veg per day.

One of the things about Sellotape is that, unlike babies, it gets stickier as it gets older. When you start work you put up posters like "You don't have to be mad to work here but it helps", which you then have to rip down pretty smartish when you're promoted to staff welfare manager. In the meantime the Sellotape has acquired the sticking power of an anally retentive barnacle and you're likely to pull down a hundredweight of plaster and the best part of your office.

It's a sad fact about Sellotape that the average person uses 32ft a year, which amounts to about half a large roll. For the metric-minded, that's half a large metric roll. The same average person takes at least six rolls a year from the stationery cupboard. That's about 800 per cent more than they need. So where does it all go? The most credible theory is that vast lengths of it are used in bizarre male bonding exercises in the sales department.

Paperclips are design classics. Unbend one and you can use it for all sorts of things – car aerial, a handy ear excavator or a useful tool for picking out staples. However, they're not actually that much use in the office. If you've got 500 memos, obviously you're not going to paperclip them all unless you run a small family business and you want to keep your grandmother totally absorbed until the end of the tax year. Important presentation documents are properly bound. They make your finished documents look smart and professional except for page number four which is still sitting quietly on the photocopier.

Pens

In the office your pen says more about you than what you write with it. Some people have one special pen that they've had for years and love so much they would turn back at passport control if they forgot it on a business trip.

As a general rule, the more expensive your pen is, the less you're likely to use it. Fat black lacquer pens that take two minutes to unscrew and have a nib with more gold than the average wedding ring are used by fat chairmen of companies to sign even fatter cheques from the company to themselves.

Most hardworking people use the humble biro, but beware of those who prefer red biros (tendency towards bossiness and petty tyranny), green biros (tendency towards eccentricity and excess body hair) and multi-coloured (mad). People who use rollerballs are generally all over the place, with no discipline or direction in their lives and with handwriting that looks like an aerial view of the passage of a stunt kite.

Office pencil users should be viewed with deep suspicion. The first kind say "let me draw what I mean", and then keep everyone waiting for half an hour while they do some blindingly obvious sketch of two overlapping circles. The second kind are the pencil whittlers who have been sharpening the same gnarled little stub since just before decimalisation. They like nothing more than licking their pencil and totting things up. The lead poisoning they inevitably suffer means they end up totting up bizarre things like train numbers or UFO sightings.

Beware managers who use rotary pencils with very fine extendable leads. They will be very surgical in their approach, writing 11.05am for their meetings instead of 11. They're usually fastidious pinched-faced people who use their rotary pencils like syringes, to inject pain into people's diaries and lives.

These days many people work with high-tech pens with fancy grips and special nibs designed to deliver a smooth flow of ink when you're pulling 5 Gs, a capability which is absolutely vital for most office workers. If, on the other hand, your pen has a colourful plastic character stuck on the top which you occasionally nibble at, this is a sure sign that promotion and worldly success is not for you. However, if the plastic character is an effigy of your boss and you're chewing its head off, you will go far.

Occasionally you come across a pen which is really nice to write with and which instantly improves your handwriting. Usually this is the pen that you've just borrowed from somebody in a meeting. Just slip it into your pocket at the end of the meeting and they probably won't notice until they're on their next business trip and they've got all the way to passport control.

Paper

Paper is the food of office life. Except for the fact that you're more likely to be consumed by paper than the other way round. If paper is the food of office life then our daily bread is the single sheet of A4 paper. On it all the most spectacular disasters in business life have been carefully written and someone has said, "Well, it looks good on paper."

Paper looks deceptively simple. There is nothing more exciting and full of potential than a blank piece of paper and yet, strangely, there is nothing quite so tedious as a piece of paper covered with a whole load of writing. That may have something to do with the fact that there's nothing more painful than having to fill a piece of paper with writing, in other words having to do some meaningful work. Life would be so much simpler if we could all just pass around blank pieces of paper bursting with potential.

Because ninety-nine per cent of work is done on A4 paper you can create quite a stir by doing your work on larger A3 paper. Or if you really want to get your message over why not copy it on to A1 paper and unfurl it on the middle of the desk of everyone who should be reading it. That'll stop them filing it away or putting it under a whole load of other rubbish. You never know, they might even read it. On the other hand, if your boss is expecting a thick report why not print it all out on tiny A6 paper, staple it together and make it into *The Little Book of Sales Figures*.

Even boring old A4 paper comes in all shapes and sizes. You can get paper "wove" that's smooth as a baby's bottom or you can get "laid" paper that's smooth as a baby's bottom after a considerable time in the bath. Professionals who want to make an impact and need to justify their exorbitant charges generally use this heavier, crinkle-cut paper in the hope that it will give their dull little letters the same sort of weighty significance as the Dead Sea Scrolls. Inadvertently, it does produce a similar effect in that the letters are usually immediately filed and forgotten about for hundreds of years.

There is a saying that a job is not finished until the paperwork is done. It's a saying that's not used much these days because most people's entire job is paperwork. It would be like saying to a shipbuilder, "The job's not over until the ship is built," which is blindingly obvious and might get you a rivet in the forehead. There is, however, a slight difference in that you can actually launch a ship and it will disappear over the horizon, whereas you can finish your paperwork and it will have multiplied and be back on your desk by the following day.

Envelopes

Be careful when someone says that they could fit all they know about what you're discussing on the back of an envelope. Given the vast range of envelopes available in the stationery cupboard, you might actually be talking to the world expert on that subject. Envelopes can be very confusingly labelled. For example, does "self-seal" mean you seal it yourself or the envelope seals itself? Get that wrong before a major mail-out and you could find yourself licking 4,000 flaps and ending up with a tongue like flypaper.

The most popular office envelope is the DL in which you put A4 letters that start Dear Sir/Madam. Sometimes these envelopes have a little window which means you have to print out your letter six times before the address is visible. As a general rule the public sector uses brown envelopes while the private sector uses white envelopes. Either way, they both want your money. If you use padded envelopes you are either sending something fragile or you are a very tactless psychiatrist.

Padded envelopes stuck down with parcel tape will survive just about anything including attempts to open them at the other end. As they're virtually impregnable, you end up stamping on them or slashing at them with a huge knife and destroying the thing inside which has been so carefully wrapped.

Some envelopes have gussets. There's nothing rude or naughty about envelopes with gussets. It is possible for grown men to ask for an envelope with a gusset without laughing. But once the post room's clear of women, there's a good half hour of raucous entertainment to be had.

Recycling

Recycling has always been an essential part of business in that most people are selling the same old things at the same old price to the same old people. These things may look new because it's the job of advertising and design to recycle fashionable art and apply it to the good old-fashioned toilet cleaner to make it seem the hippest, coolest, funkiest new thing you'd ever want to chuck down the lavatory.

Recycling in the office now involves special bins for recyclable paper. If these bins were for anything people in the office had written that was absolute rubbish, virtually all paper would be recycled. In fact a large part of the working day could be saved if printers from people's computers fed directly into these waste bins.

It's pretty certain that if you had to pay a 5p deposit on every sheet of A4 paper you used, the paperless office would spring up overnight and the internal memo would be as rare as a hairy-chested human resources director. Naturally the one other thing in the office that you have to recycle is the one thing that you most want to throw away and never see again – the photocopier toner cartridge.

Some firms are so environmentally conscious that they even recycle their people. They sack about half of them every year and then spend the rest of the year and thousands of pounds recruiting different people to do exactly the same job. Of course no one is more serious about recycling than senior management and that is why they insist on having a new car every year and also returning all your work to you untouched, unread and unnoticed so you can do it all again.

Calendars

An essential part of the clock-watcher's armoury is the wall calendar. Every January, when people return to work, a new display of these goes up in the workplace. These come in many different varieties and clearly indicate what sort of person you are. So it's best to think carefully before you get the drawing pin out.

If you have put up a calendar which has nothing but the days of the month in big black letters, perhaps with bank holidays marked in red for added excitement, then you quite obviously have the personality of a freezer bag. Those marginally better equipped in the personality department might choose to put up a calendar generously sent to them by a supplier of heating and ventilating equipment which features full-colour pictures of slimline radiators and extractor-fan outlet covers. These calendars are generally put up by people interested in nothing but knowing what the date is.

However, the majority of people put up a calendar so that they have something more attractive to look at than the back of someone's neck or the wall of their cubicle. Aside from mechanics working in small garages in Cumbria, men don't have pin-up calendars any more because they are all totally liberated from that sort of patronising sexist oppression. Instead they have moody, evocative, impressionistic black and white photographs, generally of naked women.

Many larger offices have banned any form of pin-up calendars as they can be offensive to some people. However, these restrictions never seem to include calendars such as Naughty Puppies or The Magic of Swindon, which other people may find equally offensive. Good-looking people aside, calendars give a clear and very worrying picture of our national obsessions: gaily painted traction engines, seagulls following ploughs and cats playing with wool.

As a general rule, the less busy you are, the more likely you are to have a wall calendar, a desk calendar and an egg timer on your desk. That's because the more tedious your job is, the more you count the hours and days until it's over. To avoid the danger of watching your whole life slip away, there should be calendars with pictures of bingo cards, Zimmer frames and tartan slippers to remind you what you have to look forward to at the end of your working life. In fact most people in the office are far too busy at work to have time for a calendar at all. By the end of the year, most calendars will still be showing February because that's the last time you had a moment to flick it over. That, or it's a picture of a particularly attractive extractor-fan outlet.

Desk diaries

One of the reasons why *The Country Diary of an Edwardian Lady* has become a classic is because it's not full of entries such as "Status Meeting with Derek in IT". No one has ever published a work desk diary because the more you put in it, the more boring it gets. Desk diaries are for filling and checking, not for writing and reading. Normal people don't keep their desk diaries lovingly for twenty years, dust them down and then smile wistfully as they recall that much of 2005 was spent in meetings with Derek from IT.

When your boss asks when you can do a meeting, you won't come across as a hard-working, pivotal member of the team if you open your diary and everyone gets snow-blindness from the huge expanses of white. Only chief executives have blank diaries because everyone assumes they're far too busy to have meetings. White space in a desk diary is like white space anywhere, in that it encourages vandals who write things like "Accounts meeting 8 –12" in the middle. A thin line drawn down the centre of the day will prevent this in the same way that a thin wire stretched across a ledge will stop pigeons messing it up.

Some executives pretend that they never know what they're doing from one moment to the next because their PA manages their diary. But when you actually ask the

PA if you can see the manager in question, the response is very often "Who's he?" Other executives claim they have no time in their diary for the next twelve months and yet somehow they're always at their desk to tell you this. Never trust someone who tells you they've got a window in their diary – they'll probably try to sell you double glazing.

By far the most common entry in diaries is meetings. It's frighteningly easy to completely fill up your diary with meetings so that when you eventually retire forty years later you realise that you didn't actually have any time to do your job. If you're worried that this might be happening to you, just look through your diary for the last month or so and count the times when you actually made something happen (other than a meeting).

Desk diaries are full of important information like high tides and national holidays in Canada. These tend to co-incide as Canadians get very excited about high tides. You can also find out that the currency of Malawi is the Kwacha. If, by some miracle, you needed to know what the currency of Malawi was, the last place on earth you would look is in the back of your desk diary. More inter-esting are the little bits of personal information people put in desk diaries. Look out for asterisks, which either mean PMT or an illicit liaison. In both cases it's best not to mention any changes in mood or appearance.

The information you can't really avoid in a diary is the stuff they put at the top of each page. For example, on a Monday morning it can be incredibly galling to know that it is a public holiday in Fiji. If you live somewhere as wonderful as Fiji, you don't deserve a holiday. Equally depressing are those little numbers that say 234-131. These tell you how long you have left in the year to meet your financial targets. As a general rule, once the second figure begins to look like shopping days to Christmas, you should start to think seriously about getting in some sales. Finally, at the back of the diary is the next year's year planner. You might as well draw a line from top to bottom, write in "Meeting with Derek in IT" and have done with it.

Organisers

Important people in the media have huge fat organisers that look like the leather-bound books monks used to have in the dark ages. Strangely, the people who carry them round nowadays often look like extras from *The Name of the Rose*. These media types carry round their whole life in their organisers and when they lose them they cease to exist in any meaningful way for about a year, which is a great relief to the rest of us.

However, paper-based organisers are a bit passé. You can now get very clever little electronic organisers that fit into your pocket and give you the equivalent computing power of the Belgian Ministry of Defence. But when you ask someone who has one of these organisers if they can do a meeting, it takes about three hours' continuous programming before they inform you that the only free time they had was the last three hours.

Even worse are the new personal communication tools that combine phone, fax, email and multisheet photocopier all in a unit the size of a hearing aid. People who have one of these – and for some reason they're always people doing work of minimal importance – will assure you that they can run the entire company from anywhere in the world with their little gadget. For people who can work anywhere in the world, they seem to spend an enormous amount of time in the office showing everyone their little gadget.

Calculators

Pocket calculators are everywhere these days. In fact the only place you'll never find one is in someone's pocket. Calculators are now so cheap that you can add them to anything with virtually no extra cost which is why you get things like ironing boards with built-in calculator to work out your exact ironing time per underpant.

Generally, the bigger the calculator the more insignificant the person. Truly piddling people have calculators with buttons big enough for a pig's trotter, a fat addition sign that you can operate with the side of your palm and a little roll of paper that churns out all those vital petty cash figures. If you own one of these or more than three calculators in total you are well equipped to work out just how sad you really are as a percentage of total sadness.

If you paid more than £10 for your calculator it is probably scientific. Nevertheless, it's worth paying the extra money because you never know when you're going to need to work out the fractal coefficient of the hypotenuse of xy. No one has ever used all the buttons on a scientific calculator probably because about half don't actually mean anything and are just there to impress people who failed maths GCSE.

Most calculators are now solar powered. In Britain these work for about three days a year, just long enough to let you work out average annual rainfall. The latest smart calculators interact with you. For example, the baker's calculator always throws in a couple extra just to be nice, while the finance director's calculator gives you your total and then a little message saying, "That doesn't look good, does it?" In the advertising industry, totals are automatically doubled with the message, "You can't put a price on creativity."

Photocopiers

The difference between your standard office photo-copier and the Women's Institute stall at the annual village fete is that the WI only produce jams once a year. Photocopiers have three natural states: On, Off and Out of Order. The third state is the photocopier's natural resting place between the first two states. If photocopiers were cars you would be able to drive three miles before your engine blew up and those three miles would normally be on the way to hospital for a life-saving operation.

There are now some very fancy high-tech photocopiers on the market which can give you a hundred sorted and collated documents within a minute. Sadly, the technology is so exciting that you often end up with a hundred sorted and collated blank pieces of paper because you put the original in upside-down.

There is an old and respected tradition amongst male office workers that during the office party the more excitable among them will decide that it's time to photo-copy their genitals. At this stage it's always interesting to note who pushes the enlarge button before copying. If you are going to take part in this ritual it's important that you do it before you're too drunk as you might end up using the shredder by mistake.

There are two messages that your average secretary

dreads. One is "Can you work late, Belinda?" The other is "Add Toner". Photocopier toner is specially developed to run out only on the days when you are wearing your spanking new cream silk blouse. When you have finished ever so carefully changing the toner, your silk blouse will look like a Welsh miner's donkey jacket. This fact often leads people to wonder why photocopier repairmen always turn up in natty suits. The answer is that all they ever do is lift the lid, suck their teeth and tell you that they will need to order a part that costs more than your annual salary and will be delivered shortly before you retire.

Nothing blocks human progress so stubbornly as the photocopier. Offices were happier places when machines had pistons and would respond to a good whack with a wrench by someone who used to be a stoker in a submarine. Machines, especially office ones, are now becoming increasingly pathetic, and simply won't function unless they are the centre of attention of countless technicians, consultants, sales people, service engineers, systems analysts, auditors and friendly twenty-four-hour helpline staff.

Even worse is the fact that photocopiers create work. In medieval times you didn't make a copy of something unless it was something important like the Magna Carta and even then you didn't copy it to half the country. If it weren't for photocopiers there wouldn't be in-trays and post rooms and endless paperwork. Some photocopiers are now connected to computers so that anyone in the office can run off a couple of thousand copies of a forty-page report of absolutely no interest to anyone whatsoever.

The easiest way of getting some work done and having a paperless office at the same time would be to get rid of photocopiers and other attention-seeking, labour-creating machines and then settle down with a good old-fashioned quill, pudding-basin haircut and write only what was really, really important.

Forms

Office humanity divides into two utterly separate classes: people in possession of the right form and people who are deliberately wasting everybody's time. However, being in possession of the right form is only half the battle. Having a green form when a pink form is required is also wilful and malicious corporate sabotage.

In any organisation the keeper of the form is all powerful. He can only be removed by extreme physical violence and even this requires a considerable amount of paperwork. To the form keeper, the form itself is only one basic weapon in their ceaseless struggle against personal freedom and human dignity. The heavy artillery comes in the form of rubber stamps, because of course a form without a stamp is as much use as a person without a form.

Forms are generally designed by people very low on the food chain. That's why they give you one line to fill out your entire address and half a page to clarify what sex you are.

Queen of the dockets is the multi-layered one where you keep the top copy, they keep the pink copy, the green copy goes to central filing and the bottom mauve copy goes somewhere mysterious and reappears three years later as evidence against you in an industrial tribunal.

If ever you're faced with the nightmare scenario of not

having the right form, just tell them with rock-solid confidence that of course you have the right form but that you can't possibly give it to them unless they have an appropriately stamped order form.

Business cards

Business cards are the driving licences of the business world, without which you can't get anywhere. Ninety-nine per cent of these cards are in one of two places: the top drawer of the desk of the person who owns them or the bin of the person to whom you've just given one. Top executives keep cards in thin card books and they keep a maximum of ten at any given time. If you've had a card for over three years and you've yet to use the number, it's fantastically unlikely that you're ever going to use it in the future.

There are two types of business cards. One is the cherished thing of rare beauty that you entrust to selected, fortunate people. The other is the rubbishy piece of cardboard that other pushy people hand out left, right and centre. In general non-standard-size business cards have the shelf life of bio yoghurt. No one wants to read, let alone accept, a huge business card that needs manhandling to get back to the office. A card bigger than a credit card isn't a business card, it's a greetings card and should be sent by post.

The first thing anyone looks at on the card is your title which will be Executive, Manager or Director. If you have more than three words in your job title then this is a sure-fire indication that you have a Mickey Mouse job. Take for example Executive Production Manager or Client Services Director or Deputy Prime Minister. Much better to have just one unequivocal word on your card like Chairman, Founder or God.

Recently there has been a bit of a fad for putting something on the back of your business card. This is actually slightly annoying for the recipient because that space is specifically designed for making little notes such as "on no account call this person". Many people like to give the impression that they are involved in a global business by printing their cards in Arabic or Japanese on the reverse. Often these people can't actually speak Japanese or Arabic and don't know that they have the instructions for a microwave printed on the back of their card.

The weediest, saddest thing you can do in business is give someone a card so old it has an out-of-date phone number followed by a telex number, and then say, "We're just having some new ones printed." Let's face it, you're going out of business, so don't expect them to waste one of their brand-spanking-up-to-date new cards on you. The other unspoken rule is that the more colourful your business card, the less colourful you are as a business person.

People are very proud of their business cards. In a big meeting the cool thing to do is to arrange all the cards you've been given in front of you and turn them face down whenever one of the relevant people says anything stupid. This sharpens up the remaining card givers remarkably efficiently.

8

CLOCK-WATCHING
AND DAY COUNTING

Starting work

Starting work is a very difficult period in life, and one which we all have to go through every morning of the week. However, just because you've arrived at the office, doesn't mean you have to plunge straight into work. The first essential requirement is coffee. Theoretically work can start without coffee in the same way that theoretically a car can start without petrol. Carbohydrates are also important and a couple of slices of toast and jam will markedly improve your efficiency throughout the day.

The next step is reading the mail. It doesn't matter who it's addressed to, as long as it's read. We work in the information age which means reading the papers in the morning is a vital piece of information-gathering. Naturally horoscopes need to be consulted. If you're going to make things happen in the office, there's no point in fighting against vast cosmic forces. The *Financial Times* is the only paper you can get away with reading in front of your boss, unless you work in advertising, where the *Beano* will mark you out as a dangerous intellectual.

Teamwork is never more vital than at the beginning of the day. This means checking how the rest of the team slept last night, who they slept with and how it was for them. If you're really going to clear the decks for action, make sure any outstanding gossip is dealt with at the beginning of the day. This also leaves the rest of the day clear for any late-breaking gossip.

Finally you should look at the work in hand and see whether, in the interests of the environment, energy could be saved by ignoring it. If not, check to see if you have a headache. It's amazing how you can pick up the beginnings of one if you concentrate hard enough. This might then warrant a day off, or at the very least a stroll to the pub for some fresh air.

Routine

Many people complain that work is just the same old routine, day in day out. Be grateful that it is. Just imagine if every day was like your first day at work when you knew nothing. If you had to do a different job every day you would very rapidly become a gibbering imbecile.

Routines are good. If you call them hard-earned technical skills they sound much better. In fact what you now do in one day would take a beginner a week to do. (Let's forget for the moment that having done it in one day you then take the rest of the week off.) Routines and little habits are deeply comforting. The knowledge that in your desk drawer you have two custard creams nestling pertly in tin foil to accompany mid-morning coffee can sustain you through the harsh reality of office life.

Some people have their whole day, from getting up in the morning to getting home at night, completely mapped out in such a detailed series of interlocking routines that they are, to all intents and purposes, on autopilot. These are the sort of people who know exactly where to stand on the platform in order to be where the door opens; they know precisely how much change they will need to buy their sandwich at lunch; and they circulate internal memos when they have to pass unscheduled wind. If you ever need to change anything in a company from the top down, this is the layer where changes stop dead. These tiny routines are like business ivy in that they spread rapidly, they cling on like grim death and, eventually, they kill their host organism.

As a general rule people whose days are more than fifty per cent routine are not going to go very far in the business world. They will probably be very happy and content and will view work as little parcels of unpleasantness to be got out of the way before the next scheduled custard cream. On the other hand, people who lead frenetic, stressed lives always yearn for a time when their working life will settle down to a manageable routine. This does happen eventually but it tends to coincide with grandchildren and a gift from the NHS of a new set of teeth.

Bad days

Having a bad day at the office is a double whammy because a day spent in the office is already pretty bad.

Bad days start when for no reason you decide to get out of the wrong side of the bed and accidentally step on your partner's genitals. Their immediate and total rejection of you as a human being puts you in an excellent frame of mind for the commute that's four hours long because of "service interruptions".

Greeting you at your desk is an angry note asking you for the thing you promised yesterday. When you've finished a quick bodge on that, you have to work like stink to get today's work finished for a presentation which is then cancelled at the last moment.

The time you thought you'd gained is then lost by the office bore perching one buttock on your desk and telling you lengthy stories which have had their point surgically removed. The phone call that finally interrupts this session is from your bank to say you've gone over your overdraft limit and they've bounced the cheque for your holiday. This call makes you late for a meeting with your boss about the written warning you got last week and which you've forgotten to read. He won't want to hear your excuses because he's having a bad day.

When you finally leave the building, the office sad

154

person is waiting for you because this is the night you promised to go and see his plate of cress. However, all bad days eventually come to an end and you can be sure that tomorrow will make the day you've just had look like a spring bank holiday.

Summer in the city

Every few years all work in Britain comes to a grinding halt. It's because of something that makes train strikes seem a minor inconvenience. It's something called summer. There are only three air-conditioned offices in the whole of Britain and these are reserved for visiting Americans who can only work in temperatures of between 64° and 68°. British workers regulate their temperature by becoming almost totally inert and fanning themselves with documents marked "For immediate action".

There is something that summer brings out in everyone and that is sweat. Middle managers wear shirts made out of the toxic by-products of heavy industry with labels that say "Cotton Poor. Do not wear close to the skin". Wearing these shirts is the hygiene equivalent of wrapping yourself in clingfilm and, not surprisingly, middle managers only have to lift a pen for sweat stains the size of Luxembourg to spread across their shirts in a matter of seconds. If they then decide to stand in front of a fan in an open-plan office, it has the same effect as the arrival of a dustcart full of rotting fruit and veg.

Behaviour on roads deteriorates in the heat. People open their sun roofs, sit in traffic roasting their heads for a couple of hours and then wonder why they get snappy when someone forgets to indicate. If the temperature gets absolutely stifling in the office some of the more considerate bosses will take pity on their workers and let them go home before it gets dark.

In high summer secretaries rush out to buy fans. During the winter months these fans must find their way back to the shops because at exactly the same time the following year secretaries rush out and buy more fans.

Business clothing doesn't last long in the heat. First the jackets come off, then the ties, then someone wears shorts and finally some idiot goes and spoils it all by coming to work in a G-string. And let's face it, there's nothing worse than having your annual appraisal with your boss when he's sitting in his big leather chair wearing nothing but a thong.

Birthdays

In the office, you know you're getting on a bit when you make absolutely no effort to celebrate or even mention your birthday and you're terrifically surprised if anybody else does. You shouldn't be that surprised because the modern office has all sorts of complex technical systems to remember everyone's birthday so that everyone without exception feels valued and loved. Complex spreadsheets are set up by the HR department to record everyone's birthday, buy a big card, get it circulated round the office in conditions of great secrecy and then presented to the surprised recipient. Amazingly, this is supposed to happen in offices where the average internal memo goes out two weeks late and is ignored by half its recipients and lost by the other half.

What often happens with these big birthday cards is that the first couple of people sign it in tiny writing at the bottom. Then it gets passed on to Filthy Eddy's desk, from which no document, let alone a birthday card, has ever returned. An hour before the presentation of the birthday card no one remembers where it is until finally a search and rescue team is dispatched to exhume it from Filthy Eddy's compost heap. Of course he hasn't signed it and there are still only two tiny messages at the bottom. That's when passing strangers and photocopier repairmen are press-ganged into signing the card in very big writing. If you've ever wondered who those big Best Wishes were from, now you know.

Deciding what to write in a birthday card is one of the most difficult creative tasks anyone in an office ever has to face (other than reconciling expense claims four months after they've been incurred). The obvious thing to write is Happy Birthday but that would just advertise that you had the imagination and creativity of a lump of suet. Be careful if you attempt to write a limerick. There is something about limericks that force you into outrageous obscenity especially if the first line is "There was a young man called Hank". Under pressure most people end up scribbling "Have a good one". However, even this is better than trying really hard to write something clever and witty and ending up covering half the card with absolute meaningless rubbish for someone you've met in the corridor twice.

The older you are in the office the less likely you are to want to celebrate your birthday. That's because when you reach forty everyone starts to wonder secretly why you're still a junior manager. For people between thirty and fifty, the only time you ever get to know it's their birthday is when they've just had an especially miserable day when everything goes wrong and everyone shouts at them. That's when they suddenly burst into tears and say, "And it's my birthday."

The Christmas bonus

In the office you know Christmas is on the way when you get a card from the company that supplies the glue for your carpet tiles, specially signed by Trevor, Carol and what looks like Ynathg, possibly their new Bosnian adhesive specialist. Christmas in the office is a marvellous, magical time when everyone celebrates the arrival of the long-heralded, much-discussed and universally revered figure, the Christmas bonus. Sadly not all companies have a Christmas bonus and instead employees are allowed to go home fifteen minutes early on Christmas Eve.

Adults believe in the Christmas bonus with the same passionate enthusiasm as kids under three believe in Santa Claus. You can tell how good your bonus is by seeing how long you're prepared to stay with the company to get it. If you decide in early March that you can't possibly work for that evil dwarf a moment longer, yet you're prepared to stick it out until the Christmas bonus, then in all probability it's a substantial one. The danger then is that you're so happy with your bonus and it's so cold outside, that you decide to stay on for another year, and before you know it you've been working at the same place, for the same evil dwarf, for forty years and you're the natural choice to play Father Christmas in the HR Christmas grotto.

Christmas party

Think of the person in the office that you wouldn't dream of snogging in a million years. That's the person you'll be snogging at the end of the Christmas party. Of course you can't believe that's possible, but from where you're sitting now, you probably don't believe it's possible to drink five gin and tonics, six tequila slammers and the contents of a small fire extinguisher, which you'll also be doing at the Christmas party.

The Christmas party is the one day of the year when the company mission statement comes to life. Finally, after drinking a double from every available optic, you can indulge in a bout of *openness and honesty* with the person who's been thwarting your work all year through their oafish stupidity and selfishness. Then, when you crash head first across the table where the accounts department are sitting quietly, your team can be *mutually supportive* by carrying you out to the bins at the back of the building. If you've made the mistake of inviting them to your party, you can finally *delight your customers* by reaching under their kilt and asking them if that's where they keep their oh-so-rare purchase orders.

Shortly before all this excitement happens, the managing director and some of the senior team will choose a suitable moment to show just how far they can let their remaining hair down. This involves them loosening their ties, snapping their fingers and doing a movement on the dance floor reminiscent of someone collapsing at the end of a marathon. Male managing directors will often dance with a young receptionist in a kind of accelerated waltz that looks like a bungled attempt to snatch her handbag. Throughout this exercise the receptionist will hold the managing director as if she were transporting a sock to the laundry basket.

Some companies generously provide a tab behind the bar. At least you think it's generous until Mrs Rogers orders a large sweet sherry and thereafter it's pay as you go. Most Christmas parties have themes such as Dress To Kill, Tarts and Vicars, or, a popular one amongst accountancy firms, Suit and Tie. This allows people to make a special effort and get all dressed up. This always gives rise to the tragedy of the person who goes to an enormous amount of trouble and comes in a King Kong or other completely sealed suit. They then spend the whole evening unable to get food, drink or a snog because they can't get out. Even worse, no one has a clue who's inside, so they are left completely on their own until three o'clock in the morning, when someone who has drunk themselves to the point of insanity and whose advances have been rejected by the entire company, tries to make love to them.

9

CARS, COMMUTING AND TRAVEL

Company cars

Two things separate us from our continental neighbours. One is the fact that in our early history we used to paint ourselves blue. The other is the fact that there are more company cars per head in Britain than anywhere else in the world. Company and car go together like a horse and carriage, although slightly faster, one would hope. You can't pretend to be something big in business if your car is favoured by the government because of the weediness of its size and emissions. Your car and how you handle it is the acid test of your executive potential.

Everyone loves perks and there is no perk perkier than a company car. Company cars are what all cars would be in an ideal world – they are brand spanking new and smell like it; whatever you want done to the car, even if it's getting the ashtray emptied, you can just phone someone up to take care of it (and they'll give you a courtesy car to play with while you're waiting); even more fantastic, you generally trade your company car in for a new one even before the ashtray is full; joy of joys, you can be an eighteen-year-old psychopath in a souped-up TVR and your company will pay the insurance. It's no wonder that many job ads now put "company car + salary" rather than the other way round.

Some astonishingly generous and recession-proof

companies not only give you a company car, they give you the cash and let you choose the one you want. Amazingly, some people, when given the money and carte blanche, then go out and buy an old Daewoo Turbot. You should think twice about this because your car says more about you as an executive than you could ever say yourself. For example, coupés are a big no-no in business. They over-promise and under-deliver, as do their drivers. Similarly any engine under 1997cc means you are in the charitable sector or moving rapidly in that direction. Colour of car is also important. Don't expect to get a seat on the board while you are driving anything pink, yellow, lime green or turquoise.

Sales executives hang their jacket in the back seat of their car. If you're in sales you use the little loop in the collar, but if you're in marketing you have a hanger. That's because the higher polyester content of sales suits gives a greater resistance to creasing. Also it's worth remembering that sales people don't ever wear their jackets. Having one in the car is like a Baby on Board sticker, except it means Sales Executive on Board.

If you want to get a good idea of what a company is like you need go no further than its car park. Firstly, see what cars are visible above the rest. Lots of Suzuki Vitaras, RAV4s and Daihatsu Fourtraks and you've arrived either at a design agency or a health club. If, on the other hand, the rooftops are punctuated by Previas, Espaces and Scenics, you're either at a progressive company with a balanced employment policy or you're about to have a meeting with four toddlers.

Theoretically, company cars are for the use of everyone in the company in the same way that theoretically the company is totally empowered and doesn't have a blame culture. In practice, your job either has a company car or it doesn't. When you get the company car, the first time you let someone else drive it is when the man from the leasing company comes to take it in for ashtray emptying. Sadly, if your job doesn't have a company car, no amount of asking will ever get you one. Not even if you plead and beg until you're the traditional blue in the face.

Business driving

Motorways are the natural home of the executive, especially of the high-powered sales variety. Motorways are where the lifeblood of the nation's economy flows and therefore the faster your car is flowing the more you are contributing to the economy. Driving at less than the speed limit implies a lack of commitment to growth. Top executives drive just under the speed at which you lose your licence because no licence for a sales executive is the equivalent of no coloured felt-tips for a marketing executive.

On your average weekday there are two types of car drivers on Britain's motorways. There are pensioners visiting other pensioners and there are sales reps who have three calls to make in a day and 500 miles between them. If you suddenly find yourself being flashed by a car so close behind you that you can see the driver's nostril hair, you can be fairly sure that it isn't a pensioner in a desperate rush to visit another pensioner.

Driving at a 110mph on the motorway is quality time for the rep. It's a chance to call their friends, have a bite to eat, change their shirt and relax with a good book. Occasionally smaller cars stray into the fast lane, driven by people who do less than 80,000 miles a year. This means reps have to brake hard to get down to eighty miles an hour and close enough to your back bumper for you to understand just how badly you're holding up the national economy by trespassing in their lane.

Hours of motorway driving with your body in one position means that you can stiffen up, leading to dangerous and painful cramps. To combat this you can either get out and walk around (which you can do at any time on the M25) or you can do some in-car aerobics. This involves cutting up people and then flicking V signs at them, alternating with intensive sessions of nose picking. You can also hang one arm out of the window for no apparent reason with your shirt sleeve rolled up just far enough to hang your Rolex out. This is great until your whole arm gets ripped off by another Vectra passing at 120mph.

One should always expect courtesy from other drivers and if you don't get it you should make them well aware of the deficiency by copious use of flashing lights, horn honking and expressive hand gestures. As an executive you should always bear in mind that you are a net contributor to the economy and people in smaller, older cars are probably on benefits. This gives you right of way in almost all driving situations, except where there are large trucks delivering added-value goods which someone like yourself has sold at a high margin.

Motorway service stations are meeting places for middle management. That's because none of the people in the meeting are important enough to force the other person to come to them. Instead they have to meet halfway which inevitably means the Little Chef. When you pick a service station to meet at, remember to get one with a bridge over the carriageway otherwise you're going to spend a lot of time on your mobile phone waving at the important customers on the other side of the M6.

Office car parks

Office car parks are all built to a rigid standard which requires that they have thirty per cent fewer spaces than cars. The reason why bosses get to work first is because they've got such huge cars and fat necks that they have to park first without any reversing and manoeuvring. It's left to the Ford Fiesta brigade to squeeze into the tiny little gaps the senior managers leave behind. If you use reverse gear more than five times to get into a space you probably shouldn't be parking there. Remember, it's no good sitting there in the world's smallest gap feeling all pleased with yourself if you can't then open the door.

Attached to many offices are balding men in their late fifties whose lives are dedicated to repeating the phrase, "You can't park here." The worst of these are armed with huge stickers that say "You are illegally parked" that they slap on your windscreen with industrial-strength adhesive. If you've ever wondered about that prime car parking space that's always empty and always has a cone in the middle of it, that one belongs to him and no, you can't park there.

Some people, usually sales reps, block you in and leave their keys at reception. Naturally they are the same people that have fixed every kind of immobiliser and security device to their Vauxhall Vectra so that people won't steal it and undermine their masculinity. That's why when you attempt to unlock it and move it you won't get within five yards of it before enough sirens are going off to make anyone over sixty head for their air-raid shelter. If your company has lots of sales reps who all drive Vauxhall Vectras there's a real danger that you'll drive off in the wrong car and only realise your mistake when you're stuck in a five-mile tailback on the M62 with only *Brass Band Memories* for company.

Company car parks can still be very hierarchical, with special places reserved for chairman, director etc. You can guarantee your own spot with a sign saying "Office Nerd" or you can have the chairman's spot by replacing his sign with 'Official Receiver'. Occasionally the best spot in the car park is reserved for employee of the month. If you walk to work or take the bus you can guarantee that you'll be employee of the month about seven times a year so the spot is kept clear for the chairman. In some car parks you will see registration plates attached to the wall to allocate spaces. In fact these are usually number plates embedded in the wall by extremely bad drivers. Finally, don't forget that if you work in the office past eight in the evening on a regular basis, you are legally entitled to a residents' parking permit.

Commuting

If rats were to conduct experiments into human behaviour, instead of using the traditional maze they would most probably choose to observe us in a crowded commuter train. After a period of observation, a number of patterns would emerge. For example, the seemingly random distribution of passengers on the morning platform is actually a microscopically exact science so that the passenger merely has to extend their arm to open the required door. Behind this door will be the precise seat that will carry them to the exact spot they need to alight in order to be directly opposite their exit on arrival.

Naturally, commuters will often find themselves sitting opposite precisely the same person every morning. In a larger research project, rats would note that commuters spend more time opposite the person in the train than opposite their partner at home. This can have two effects. Firstly, it occasionally happens that you bump into this person somewhere other than the train. As they are so familiar you stop and engage them in conversation. It soon becomes apparent that neither of you know the first thing about the other apart from what newspaper they read. The following morning you realise who that person is and, instead of introducing yourself and becoming good friends, you move your platform position by six feet with the result that you never, ever meet again. Or, alternatively, the person opposite ends up sitting opposite you at home.

The three most unpopular things on commuter trains are hamburgers, mobile phones and teenagers. That's because each, in its different way, breaks the cardinal rule of commuting, which is that you must not intrude on your neighbour in any way: a hamburger smells offensive to anybody who isn't eating it; a mobile phone sounds offensive to anybody who isn't using it; and teenagers are offensive to anybody who isn't one.

It is a cast-iron rule of commuting that the newspaper of the person sitting next to you is always more interesting than your own, even though you are reading exactly the same newspaper. Sometimes, when they've finished their newspapers, business executives use the train to read office paperwork of numbing banality. When was the last time you couldn't wait for your neighbour to turn the page of their business report so you could see what happened next?

Many commuters choose to read books on the train. Women tend to read books about relationships. Glance across at one of the pages and you will read something like, "I love you, Barry, but I'm just not ready." Men, on the other hand, will be reading books about killing with lines like, "There's no pin in that grenade, Barry." Some people read science fiction on the train but no one sits close enough to them to see what sort of lines they have in their books.

International business

It's one of the big mysteries in corporate life how European multinationals operate successfully when most of their meetings involve people from countries that have little in common other than a shared distaste for America. It's especially mysterious, given the fact that for some reason everyone in these meetings tries as hard as they can to conform to their most grotesque national stereotypes. Nothing makes the French more French than when they are sitting between the Germans and the British.

In these meetings the French will always insist on discussing the philosophical purpose behind everything, even if the meeting is about developing new worming pills for cats. The Germans will then tell the meeting in exhaustive detail how they do things in Germany and why it would be better for Europe in general if everyone did it their way. As soon as the Belgians or Dutch say anything the Germans and the French will immediately start talking amongst themselves and work out a cosy solution that suits them both. Meanwhile the Italians will be sitting very carefully to make sure they don't put unnecessary creases in their suits and then will suddenly get very excited about a small point and threaten to walk out. The British will be very reasonable and understanding, make lots of jokes and find themselves at the end of the meeting totally isolated.

In fact these multinational meetings are very like the European Community in miniature. All parties try to get along for the sake of economic progress but really everyone wants to go home where things are done properly and you can get a decent sausage.

If you travel a lot on international business you normally get frequent flyer points. Business flyers collect frequent flyer points like people used to collect football cards. This is a bit of a mystery, because business flyers are always complaining how much they hate flying and are bored to tears by it, while at the same time collecting like mad to claim their free eighteen-hour flight to Alaska. As a frequent flyer you will also be entitled to use the club lounges at airports. These are well worth getting excited about as they're packed with free papers worth well over 50p, all the mineral water your bladder can hold and all the executives with shiny trouser-bottoms your heart desires.

Executive hotels

Many business travellers claim that hotels are homes from home. That's utter nonsense because hotels are nothing like home. For a start you get a bed the size of a squash court that could still have the previous occupant in and you'd be none the wiser. Also the pillows on the bed are made of some sort of high-pressure foam that won't let your head sink into them unless you're wearing a lead-lined night cap. New smart technology means the hotel always knows who you are and what you're doing so that when you switch on the television in bed a little message pops up, "Good Evening Mr Hollingsworth, thank you for choosing The Adult Movie Channel. We thought you might."

There are three kinds of hotel for the travelling executive: the inner-city battery hotel with 500 identical cubicles; the country hotel with hunting prints and worn carpets; and the motorway service-station lodge with CCTV and five locks on the door. Wherever they stay it is a point of honour for the travelling executive to find their hotel armed with nothing but a map printed from the web. A slip of the wrist while typing in the postcode may mean spending the night in a lay-by. But that's infinitely preferable to asking for directions.

Your room key will normally be a plastic card. If it's a

metal key you are in a bed and breakfast. If it's a metal key with a key fob the size of a sideboard door, you are in a country hotel. There are two ways of finding your room. One is to follow all the little signs that say Rooms 143-194. After a day on the road it can often be quite difficult to work out whether 174 is within this range or not. The other way to find your room is to listen for the sound of a very loud television doing its best to drown out four screaming children. Your room will be next door.

Hotel rooms come in two temperatures: roasting hot and scalding hot. Fortunately hotels understand this and put an extra blanket in the wardrobe just in case you're feeling chilly. In upmarket hotels you might have a room with air-conditioning. Some of these are so noisy they might as well be called flight simulators. Most air-conditioning units have an extremely complicated set of controls that allow you to turn it on or off. If you turn it on as soon as you arrive, your room will generally be comfortable shortly before you leave.

Things that everyone has at home cause great excitement in hotel rooms: "Look, there's a little kettle, that's fantastic!" For women the most essential part of any hotel is the hair dryer. Sadly most hotel hair dryers have the power of an old man's dying breath. Also beware of the minibar in your room. This is the most profitable part of the whole hotel and just opening the door and glancing at the peanuts adds at least two digits to your bill.

In good hotels, room service arrives in your room in seconds, whether you want it or not. Getting them out of your room is another matter as they will lurk around for ever asking pointless questions like "Have you come far?" until you empty out your wallet for a tip. This makes breakfast in your room extremely difficult as there's nothing worse than trying suavely to tip someone when you're half comatose and stark naked. The one thing that will get someone in your room faster than room service is hanging out the "Do Not Disturb" sign. This tells the voyeurs on the hotel staff when and where to burst in, causing maximum embarrassment to you and your HR director.

Many executives like to have a room-service breakfast. However, the chances of getting exactly what you order is roughly the equivalent of finding a male-voice choir in your bathroom. To order your breakfast you fill in a little card and hang it outside your door. Someone collects these cards late at night and then destroys them all. They then randomly allocate breakfast items. It's only when you sit down to eat you realise that a vital ingredient is missing such as a spoon. You could call room service again but by the time you get your spoon your meeting will be starting.

Wake-up calls should never be organised until you're sitting on your bed and have begun to bond with it. Wake-up calls arranged from this position are guaranteed to be half an hour later than the ones you organise in reception. Those who really know about hotels don't bother with wake-up calls because what happens is you normally wake up half an hour before your wake-up call and then can't take a shower because you know that as soon as you get your head under the water the phone will ring.

Most hotels these days operate an express checkout system. This is where you check out so fast that you forget your camera, your trousers and your briefcase full of vital business documents. If you check out in person you'll generally be asked if you want your credit card slip stapled to your bill. If you think that's a sad question, think how sad the people are who feel passionately about stapled/not stapled. And what's most sad is that's exactly the sort of person you're about to meet on your key business trip.

Trouser presses

The acid test of whether you are a businessman as opposed to a working man is if you have intimate working knowledge of a trouser press. Most men, business or otherwise, get through life perfectly happily without having their trousers pressed, but put a man in a hotel bedroom and suddenly he starts putting his whole wardrobe through the press to get those razor-sharp creases so vital to business success.

The sales force for trouser presses must be among the most persuasive in the world because of all the things you could really do with in a hotel room (like a decent-sized mug or a pair of slippers or a selection of crisps), they've managed to sell in a machine which takes the creases out of the back of your trousers. It's not even as if you can hide the thing away in a drawer – it just stands there in the corner like a little upright man saying, "I want to press your trousers."

In truth the trouser press is in-room entertainment for bored executives. Because there is a trouser press there, you simply have to press your trousers. You don't pay through the nose for your room without coming out of it with a crease in your trousers, no sir. If the hotel left a courtesy oxyacetylene torch for the convenience of guests, businessmen would probably find a whole load of spot welding that suddenly needed doing in their luggage.

Businessmen often only have one suit when they travel so when they arrive in a new hotel room the first thing they do is slip their trousers in the press. They then have to sit around in their underpants for exactly thirty minutes. During this half-hour, they will have approximately eighteen visits from room service, maintenance men and other passing strangers. Although women wear the trousers these days they are not so stupid as to want a trouser press in their hotel room. Only a man could think that heating up his trousers for thirty minutes will enhance his chances of business success. That's why the ultimate turn-off for a woman in the bedroom at home, apart from the traditional pant-sock combination favoured by British manhood, must be the sight of a trouser press in the corner. Thinking about it, the origin of this pant-sock combination may well be the many hours businessmen spend dressed like this waiting for their trousers to be pressed.

10

FIXTURES
AND FITTINGS

Office space

Open-plan offices are only open when you're standing up. When you sit down you might as well be in an airing cupboard. The view from your desk says a lot about you. If it's a panoramic view of a major world city, then you're either enormously successful or you're looking at a postcard pinned to your cubicle wall one foot from your face. It's a sad fact of corporate life that the less time you spend at your desk the better your view will be. That's why the chairman, who thinks a work station is where he catches the train from, has a beautiful soothing view. Whereas if you spend seventy hours a week stuck at your desk, you probably have a view equivalent to putting a cardboard box on your head.

The most irritating view in the office is the back of the person in front. If all you ever see of someone is the back of their head, you will end up hating them and the stupid little mole halfway up their neck. But the worst view of all is your boss, because if you can see them, they can see you. This means you will have to simulate meaningful activity for hours at a time and speak to all your friends on the phone as if they are important business contacts.

When people move offices, there is always an unseemly bun-fight to secure a desk by a window. Having a window is great, especially if it's one you can climb out of with no one noticing (don't try this if you're on the thirty-third floor). Having a window is not so good if you look straight out on to a wall on which someone has written, "We're all going to die." Top managers who want to communicate effectively should try putting signs outside their building, given how much time their staff spend staring out of the window.

One of the benefits of being the managing director is that your office has the best view in the whole building. Managing directors need all this space and quiet because, in all fairness, they have to do a lot of top-level strategic thinking. Everyone knows how it's impossible to think straight when seven phones are ringing, when four people want to see you and when someone at the next desk is doing Elvis impressions – because everyone, bar the MD, has to do it.

Desks and chairs

There are two chairs in the managing director's office. One is four foot wide, is made from the hide of a Charolais bull and looks like the palm of King Kong. This is not the one you sit in when you go in for your annual carpeting. Your chair is the little plastic one which forces you to sit bent double and is on the point of complete collapse, which is exactly the feeling it's supposed to induce. Big boardrooms generally have lots of huge swivel chairs. If it's your first board meeting, you won't make much of an impression if the rest of the board walk in and you're spinning round in your chair pretending you're in *The Magic Roundabout*.

Beware offices with sofas. You are either in the HR department, where they like to make you comfortable while they fill out your P45, or you're in an advertising agency where they like to make you comfortable before showing you a creative campaign that could have been written by a chimp in a flotation tank.

A desk covered in papers and reports and unfinished sandwiches means that you are an inefficient, fly-blown slob who should be sacked. A sparkling clean desk with nothing on at all means that you are an inefficient, fly-blown slob who has just been sacked. A good way of deciding whether your desk is untidy is to wait until the phone rings. If you can hear it but can't see it, then your desk probably needs more than a light dusting. Some companies run a clean desk policy, which means that no one can leave work unless their desk looks like the flight deck of the Ark Royal. In practice, clean desk policies usually translate into full drawers.

You can tell a lot about the company you work for by the desks it has. If your desk has a wooden lid and a little ink well in the corner, your company is unlikely to be at the cutting edge of the technological revolution. On the other hand, if your desk looks like Houston ground control you're probably at the cutting edge of British technology and therefore almost certainly facing imminent redundancy.

Hot desking is a pernicious modern phenomenon where nobody has their own desk. Instead you have to find a clear desk to park yourself at the beginning of the day in exactly the same way as you have to find a spot in the car park to park your car. A good way of cooling down a hot desk is to leave a picture of your family on the desk, a spare jacket on the seat and a half-eaten sandwich in the middle. Or work continuously, never leave your seat and end up as finance director.

Doors

Doormats have had a very bad press over the years but they provide a vital function in the office. That's because no one ever wipes their feet going into an office. If receptionists sometimes appear a little grumpy, it's probably because you've just left a trail of mud, oil, grime and filth all the way across their beautiful foyer carpet. At home you're well within your rights to ask people to take their shoes off. In the office this is not possible as the marketing director would be forced to remove his Cuban heels and everyone would realise he was a midget.

People never wipe their feet going into an office because generally their mind is on other things like, for example, how to get into the office in the first place. Entering an unfamiliar building can be one hell of a palaver. Revolving doors give rise to great fear and loathing, and with good reason. Manually operated ones generally need a good shoulder barge to get them moving but then pick up speed pretty rapidly. That's why you should never enter a revolving door when somebody is trying to go out the other way. Both pushing at the door at the same time generates enough force to move the main propeller of a cruise ship and will immediately hurl you across reception, at the same time catapulting the person you've come to meet out into the car park. On the other hand, applying too little force leaves the door precisely where it is, with your face jammed up against the glass.

Automatic revolving doors are equally loathsome because they have been specifically programmed to play games with you which undermine your business credibility and personal dignity. If you get within a foot of either the back or the front of your little segment, the whole thing shudders to a stop, leaving you in a little glass case for everyone sitting in reception to stare at. This stopping and starting is incredibly patronising behaviour on the part of the door and implies that you can't walk round safely by yourself. In circumstances like this, just pretend the door is manually operated and give it a really good shove.

Many security-conscious companies now have an additional obstacle to making a dignified entrance to their building. They have erected a little turnstile which you walk up to, swipe your security card, lift up your briefcase and then get stopped dead by a steel bar at groin height. When you've straightened up you then have to resurrect someone from security, who lets you through the little gate at the side which he always leaves open anyway.

What these security-conscious companies don't realise is that the absolutely foolproof way of preventing everybody, including your staff, from ever getting into the office is to have a big sign on both doors which says PULL.

Fridges

The coldest and most inhospitable places on earth are the Antarctic and the office fridge. In a crisis, you would survive longer on the contents of the Antarctic.

There are three types of milk in the fridge: the first is honest-to-goodness whole milk for normal hardworking people; the second is semi-skimmed milk for slightly faddy, neurotic people who insist on a low-fat beverage with their doughnut; the third kind is skimmed milk, favoured only by hollow-faced office puritans and finance directors, for whom skimming is a way of life. There is a fourth substance in the fridge called ex-milk. This is milk that has evolved through cream, butter and cheese to become radioactive sludge. Don't sniff this milk if you have important work to do.

Milk only gets into the fridge because there is generally one person good enough to actually buy it. You would have thought that everyone would like this person. Far from it. In fact everyone ignores this person until one day they forget the milk and then everyone hates them.

People who have been shopping at lunch-time like to store their food in the fridge until they can take it home. That's fine, but don't ever take it out of the carrier bag because there are men in every office who believe that an unopened chocolate gateau in the fridge was bought specifically for them.

One thing you'll always find in a fridge is the scribbled note, such as, "Was that chocolate fudge cake anybody's? Call Helen." If you move fast enough, you'll probably catch Helen finishing the whole cake off to compensate for a particularly brutal appraisal. In larger offices you can get involved in quite lengthy fridge note correspondence, sometimes even leading to romance. Look out for the telltale signs of frostbite.

For bosses, the fridge is a subtle way of checking staff pay levels. Shelves groaning with smoked salmon, caviar and strawberries call for swingeing pay cuts. Alternatively, longlife milk and a tin of shoe polish might prompt bosses to raise pay to the minimum wage or even to turn the fridge on.

Eventually, every fridge needs defrosting. During defrosting you often find the perfectly preserved remains of someone who was rumoured to have taken early retirement. They will probably be frozen in the position in which they died, with their nose sniffing a bottle of ex-milk.

First aid kits

The office first aid kit is like the G spot: everyone knows it's there, but no one can quite put their hands on it. Like the G spot, finding the first aid kit can prove to be a disappointment. For some reason they all seem to comprise seven large triangular bandages. It's estimated that UK offices have more bandages in storage than were used in the entire Crimean War. These would be handy if the building collapsed in an earthquake but otherwise they're completely useless. Who is ever going to say "I've dislocated my collar bone. Don't worry about the ambulance, just pass me one of those triangular bandages and I'll press on with this report"? No one unless they've also received a hefty knock on the head.

All offices are supposed to have a trained first aider. This tends to be the office leper with the thermonuclear halitosis. Unfortunately, people would sooner volunteer for open-heart surgery from the maintenance man than mouth-to-mouth with him. A much more useful job for the office first aider would be to go round to the homes of people who were off sick and see if they were as ill as they sounded on the telephone.

Many first aid kits come with helpful emergency guidelines such as what to do in the event of a tidal wave or an all-out chemical or biological attack. What they don't do is give hints on the real office emergencies such as a broken fingernail or a boss with post-lunch snappiness. It's probably just as well, as the solution would no doubt involve several large triangular bandages.

Real first aid kits should be kept in the office fridge and consist of a number of ice-cold gin and tonics. If you insist on having a first aid tin these should be packed with headache pills, powerful anti-depressants and disposable nappies for use in annual appraisals. Of course what's in a first aid kit is largely academic, because when it comes to locating it in an emergency, you've got more chance of finding the Holy Grail.

Pot plants

Pot plants are to offices what goalkeepers are to football: they look ridiculous and their only function is to get in your way. Fortunately, out of the nation's seven million office plants, 4.5 million are currently dead or terminally ill. Most die of passive smoking, because every cigarette stubbed out in a pot plant takes three weeks off its life – except for tobacco plants, which absolutely thrive on it.

Office plants are among the hardiest in the world because, apart from smoking twenty a day, they are fed on a diet of coffee, tea, oxtail soup and an annual dose of Christmas party urine. They also have to cope with the gardening efforts of the cleaners who give them a daily spray of furniture polish to keep them looking nice.

There is one very healthy and beneficial aspect to pot plants. They take in noxious gases and recycle them as valuable oxygen. In this respect they are completely the opposite to the boys who work in the post room, who take in valuable oxygen and recycle it as noxious gases. Plants grow if you talk to them nicely, which is why plants in HR departments do so well. This also explains why so many bosses have stunted little bonsai trees on their desks as nothing's going to grow very much in that atmosphere.

Office lifts

Office lifts are mini laboratories for the study of human embarrassment. That's because it's generally very difficult to make polite conversation with someone who is within an inch of the farthest tendrils of your nasal hair. On the other hand some women find lifts an excellent place to give themselves a total makeover, highlight their hair and wax their bikini area in the space of ten floors. This may be very convenient for them, but it can be embarrassing for everyone else in the lift.

If you want to know whether a company is going up in the world you need look no further than its lifts. Any company where the walls of the lifts are carpeted is a company on the royal road to receivership; any company with glass lifts on the outside of the building is probably built on some Enron-style accounting; and any company with more lifts than floors is unlikely to be much good at any sort of business.

In some quaint old lawyers offices they like to retain the ancient wooden lifts with the metal cage doors that are so heavy you can only open them if you're the sort of person who regularly bench presses over 300lbs. Once inside you push the button and the lift hurtles upward at a floor every ten minutes. If you get stuck in one of these lifts never push the emergency button, as this just severs the hairy old rope that's holding the lift up.

New lifts have electronic voices that patronise you by saying "Going up" when you've just got in at the ground floor. What would be better is a voice that said really useful things like, "Would the man in the green tie get out at the next floor for the convenience and safety of the remaining passengers." Modern lifts also have extremely sensitive doors which can be held open by the frailest of old ladies. You have to wedge their whole body in sideways, but it can be done.

Newton's laws of physics do not apply to lifts. When you go up to the managing director's floor you still get a sinking feeling and when you come back down you feel uplifted (if you've still got your job).

Toilets

It has taken man hundreds of thousand of years to evolve from a primitive savage to a high-tech master of the universe. To trace this evolution in reverse, simply step from any modern office into the gentlemen's toilet. Men can put a Cruise missile through a bedroom window in Baghdad yet can't point Percy at the porcelain at point-blank range.

There is a saying that you can tell a lot about the morale of a company by the state of its lavatories. If this is true, then the whole of French industry must be in a state of deep and continuous depression. The lavatories in city institutions, on the other hand, are so spotless that you wonder if bankers ever have bowel movements. Knowing how difficult it is to get anything out of a banker, it's probably safe to assume they don't.

You can learn a lot about your colleagues in the wash-room. For example, you can get a little pipsqueak from accounts who doesn't touch tea or coffee all day, who has one diet Ribena for lunch, and yet pees like a horse for well over five minutes. In general, nothing halts the free flow of urine faster than the chief executive pulling up in the stall next to you and saying, "How's your career coming along, Michael?" Especially if your name isn't Michael.

On your way out of the loo you can dry your hands in one of three ways. There is the roll on the wall that only lets you pull down one foot of towel for every ten thousand people who use it. Or there's the hot-air blower which has the power of a ninety-year-old asthmatic and cuts out while your hands are still dripping. Occasionally you get a really powerful blower that you foolishly point upwards and exit looking like Ken Dodd. Finally there's what you do when there are no towels or blowers at all. Your only option is to wave your hands around briskly like you're trying to get rid of a very sticky plaster. This is normally when the chief executive strolls in and marks you down as an absolute crackpot.

Ladies' lavatories are a lot like women's handbags – nothing special on the outside, but a whole world of fascination, mystery and excitement on the inside. Men have always wondered what goes on inside the Ladies, because if you happen to be walking past when the door is just closing, you can always hear women laughing and chatting and doing all sorts of marvellous fun things.

Men generally imagine that inside the Ladies there's a pool table, jukebox, fridges full of exotic cocktails, beauty therapists applying seaweed to women's faces, wall-to-wall shag-pile carpet, piped music, the aroma of lavender and primrose, large posters of George Clooney on the walls and blown-up copies of *Cosmopolitan* articles entitled "How to humiliate men in the bedroom and the boardroom".

Of course there are other reasons why queues form, and one is that women will do anything to avoid sitting down in the loo. They hang with both hands from the light fitting, or wedge themselves between the partition walls or use all available loo rolls to re-paper the cubicle from floor to ceiling. It doesn't help that there is only ever one cubicle in the Ladies. That, of course, is because the rest of the space is taken up with exercise bikes, jacuzzis, Clinique counters etc.

11

EATING, DRINKING AND CLOTHING

Coffee and tea

In an open-plan office there is a ritual where everyone waits hours for the first person to say, "Who wants a coffee?" That person then finds themselves in the kitchen for the rest of the day following the little chart that says "Diane, white with two Nutrasweet and half a custard cream". Naturally everyone hates vending-machine coffee, but there's one thing that everyone hates more and that's the "I don't drink coffee, I'll have a rhubarb tea" brigade.

"White no sugar" is the standard office request for a beverage. It announces that you're a normal, decent person, averagely concerned with their health, but not above a modicum of stimulation. Anything else and you begin to make statements about yourself. For example, if you want tea instead of coffee in the office, generally it's true to say that you are a nicer, more relaxed person. Unless, that is, you want herbal tea, which means you are too nice, too relaxed, probably don't like the word profit and unlikely to be any good in a sales capacity. Earl Grey says two things about you: one is that you are or want to be posh and the other is that you like your tea to taste like lightly soaped dish-water.

Some very progressive companies have cappuccino bars where fresh coffee is always available along with a selection of freshly baked delicacies. This is a popular place to meet, especially among the receivers who come in to wind up the company for not controlling their costs.

Vending machines

In primitive cultures manhood is sometimes tested by drinking a brew siphoned from the backside of the fanged dung bat. In our culture this has been replaced by the coffee vending machine. All the drinks have numbers such as White Without Sugar 402. This number generally refers to the atomic half-life of what the machine dumps into your cup.

Vending machines fill up your cup to within one millimetre of the brim. The cup itself is so flimsy that the slightest pressure wangs it out of shape and spurts coffee down your boss's shirt. Even if you keep the cup together, by the time you reach your desk it feels as if the top three layers of skin on your fingers have melted off.

If you're a smoker, nothing makes coffee taste better than a long drag on a cigarette. If you're a non-smoker, nothing makes coffee taste worse, especially if you swallow the butt someone dropped in it earlier. Anyone who works in an office will have noticed the strange gravitational pull between coffee and the document that you shortly have to present to your boss. Human reactions are never quicker than when a coffee is about to spill. At the last moment it can often be knocked clear of the document and straight into the keyboard of your computer.

Only people who come in from outside to clean or fix

things have two sugars in their tea. That's why when you're in a meeting room and they bring in the teas and coffees, you never get those really useful glass containers with the silver spout that can pour huge spoonfuls into your mug. This is probably a good thing, because given the rinky-dink little cups they have on the tray with the little shell-like handles you get your finger stuck in, one spoonful of sugar would fill half the cup. Then there's the additional problem that you can't stir anything in a meeting because while your big boss is explaining the precipitous drop in sales figures, no one wants to hear you clattering away like a little spin dryer.

The other extreme is people who take their coffee black. These people are without exception hard-nosed, heartless, square-jawed business ball-breakers who can manage just about anything in business apart from opening those little pots of UHT milk. One last word of warning: if you come across someone who has black coffee and two sugars they are likely to be severely dysfunctional and have violent mood swings. Part of the reason for this is that they will have spent a lifetime in business never getting the drink they asked for.

Biscuits and snacks

The type of biscuit you prefer in the office is a dead giveaway to the sort of business you work in and, equally important, to what sort of person you are. For example, it will come as no surprise to learn that Jammie Dodgers are the number one biscuit in both advertising and estate agencies.

Wholewheat digestives are consumed by serious-minded people such as VAT inspectors or health and safety officers. Offering them a chocolate digestive in return can be construed as an attempt to bribe them. At the other end of the spectrum are the pink wafers that tend to pop up in design consultants and interior decorators. If you are offered pink wafers by a civil engineering firm, check the way they mix their concrete.

More exotic biscuits are found in more specialised environments; fig rolls are popular with Persian carpet wholesalers and also drain-cleaning operatives. Successful small businessmen tend to gravitate towards Rich Shorties while ageing football managers generally opt for Garibaldis. Rice cakes and rusks are only eaten in the offices of small pressure groups who hate everyone, including themselves. If you have to have a meeting with them take a packet of Chocolate HobNobs and cheer them all up.

Snacks are the in-flight refuelling of office life. Women who have a low-calorie lettuce leaf for lunch will often have had enough snacks in the morning to sustain a small Turkish weightlifter.

Of all snacks, chocolate is the most important. Women have a deeper and more complex relationship with chocolate than they do with men. That's because with chocolate you get more taste, more immediate response and you can use your teeth.

Any office which allows you to have a bacon butty to start work is clearly deeply committed to the welfare of its workforce. Sadly it also means a maintenance team whose sole job is to remove tomato ketchup from computer keyboards.

The National Audit Office has statistically proven that habitual biscuit dunkers are low achievers. It's a bizarre habit, as very often one half of the biscuit falls into the coffee. This has nothing to do with dunking skill because even if you dipped an iron bar into vending-machine coffee half of it would dissolve and fall off.

Staff canteen

In an office you know it's lunch-time when your stomach starts making more noise than your boss. Getting away from the boss at lunch-time is great as long as this doesn't mean going to the staff canteen.

In job advertisements you often see "subsidised canteen" offered as some sort of inducement. Unless it's followed by "free health insurance", steer clear of the job. British food has little to recommend it at the best of times and when you try to serve a meal at 30p a head it's not surprising that you end up with the culinary equivalent of trench foot on your plate.

Naturally Shepherd's Pie is a big favourite with canteens. For vegetarians they can take the meat out and call it Country Pie and for something really exotic they can add curry powder and call it Dragon Pie. Lasagne is Shepherd's Pie with pasta instead of potato and Ocean Pie is Shepherd's Pie with fish. This is normally served on Friday so that people will at least have the weekend to forget all about it.

These days a lot of catering is contracted out to customer-focused private catering companies. 'Customer focused' means they don't take their eyes off you when you're helping yourself to chips in case you take too many and jeopardise the dividend for shareholders. Their big secret is "portion control", which means instead of being able to slosh ketchup all over your lasagne they give you one sachet to squeeze, which yields up little more than a good-size blackhead.

In the old days there used to be a separate restaurant for executives. Nowadays it's all democratic and open plan and you can sit wherever you want, which of course happens to be any table which doesn't have any executives on.

Business drinking

Alcohol and business don't mix. Which is why if you like a drink you really shouldn't bother with work. Excessive drinking at work makes you feel sociable, light-headed and confident that you can do anything. In other words, it makes you feel like you work in sales. The day after, when you feel like the whole world is a grim, head-crushing torture chamber, it makes you feel like you work in IT.

Drinking at lunch-time is a great pleasure not only for those who do it, but also for those who work for those who do it. That's because afternoons become the time when you can get your expenses signed, your holiday approved and your salary upped just by lifting your boss's head off their desk, smiling sweetly and putting the appropriate form in front of their nose. Of course when we're talking about lunch-time drinking, we don't mean half a lager shandy – we mean drinking so much you can't find your office from the pub across the street.

Certain industries drink more heavily than others. The computer industry is virtually teetotal because computers have a very low tolerance of incomprehensible input from smashed human. In industries such as PR, where clarity of thinking is a professional disadvantage, drinking is mandatory until the desired level of mindless bonhomie is achieved. Saddest of all are the boozy old lags who sit around for hours broadcasting their personal inadequacies in a loud voice to anyone who will listen. Yet somehow these board meetings always seem to sober up at the critical moment and vote themselves wallet-bending share options.

Most people like to have a drink after work, especially on Friday when it doesn't matter how revolting you feel the following day. After-work drinks show you where you really stand in the office. If everyone says they're going down The White Hart and at closing time you're still all alone nursing your fourth half-pint, you can be pretty sure that the rest of the company are whooping it up at The Swan.

It's an absolute rule that the person who earns least in the office will be the first person to get his wedge out and buy a round. He is also the first to get absolutely hammered and say something so offensive that he gets passed over for a rise for the seventh year running.

Just because you're the boss, don't think you can join in the fun. Six minutes after you've arrived at The Swan, everyone will suddenly have to leave to babysit. This babysitting will commence down at The Rose and Crown five minutes later.

After-work drinking is divided into three phases: the first is general whingeing at how bad the company is, how dreadful your customers are and why your boss is a plonker; the next phase, after the second pint, is an intense bitch about the person in The Swan; the third phase is when people with a family go home, leaving the sad single people to drink to the point of insanity, where a kebab seems like a good idea.

Finally, it's another absolute rule that the last two people to leave the pub are having an affair and will go off somewhere to do something way beyond their job descriptions.

Smoking

In the Fifties, if you worked you smoked and if you didn't like it you could nip outside and get a lungful of smog. These days the only smoking offices are small jobbing printers where the boss smokes an old pipe, kippering the entire workforce.

Smoking is a very good way of bonding with people. You can share an intimate cigarette in a way that you could never share an intimate muesli bar. By the way, never offer a cigarette to someone who's eating a muesli bar. It's a lifestyle thing.

You can tell if there's a smoker in a meeting because they'll be drumming on the table within five minutes and insisting on a break to "get some fresh air". Much more irritable and aggressive, however, are the virulent anti-smokers who regard smoking as an assault with a deadly weapon.

Smoking is a great excuse not to work. A non-smoker standing under a gutter for no reason would rightly be called a slacker. Time spent smoking is not made up for by post-nicotine incisiveness, as a cigarette is generally followed by a cup of coffee and analysis of the gossip generated whilst standing outside.

Cigarettes are bad for your health. Standing outside in your shirt sleeves in all weathers is inviting pneumonia.

Smoking outside also means you have a front entrance that looks like someone's just emptied their car ashtray on the pavement. Smokers are therefore forced to drop their stubs in their pockets, which sometimes leads to the hugely entertaining spectacle of someone being set alight during an important telephone sales call.

Work clothes

In business, what you wear says more about you than you can ever say yourself. Decisions you make standing in front of the mirror first thing in the morning are more important than any decisions you'll make in the office.

The traditional male suit is like a woman in that the closer it is to you, the better it feels. However, unlike a woman, single-breasted is always preferable to double-breasted. Only wide boys, lawyers and Tory candidates wear double-breasted suits. When it comes to selection of cloth, there is a choice between very dark grey and very dark blue. Purple, taupe or red suits are for children's television presenters and account men in small design agencies with very poor creative work.

There are two types of ties in business. The first is the recessive, sober pattern in six-fold silk. The other is a tie-shaped piece of Indian restaurant wallpaper which hangs briefly round your neck before finding its natural resting place in a charity-shop window. Knots on ties should never be bigger than the head of the wearer. Similarly a tie should never be wide enough to cover both nipples at once.

Men in the office have one place to demonstrate their sartorial flair and that is in their choice of cufflinks. The rule here is that if it would also look good as an earring, it's not an appropriate business cufflink.

You can wear sensible black lace-ups in business or you can wilfully decide to wear some brown suede loafers and shunt your career into a siding called Total Failure. You can also wear sandals in business as long as your business is in IT software development and you don't want to have a meaningful relationship with anything that doesn't have Intel Inside.

One of the secrets for being a top executive is you should never be caught wearing the jacket of your suit. There are three places for your jacket to live: hanging in the back of your car, over the back of your chair in the office and in the wardrobe of the business-class compartment of a Boeing 777. Wearing a suit jacket makes you look slightly stiff, with an accountancy background. Not wearing your jacket makes you look hard-working, and approachable with a slightly creative background.

Working women often fling open their wardrobe in the morning and complain that they have nothing to wear. Yet you never see women in the office wearing nothing, so something's not quite right there. When men fling open the wardrobe in the morning they see the same suit they have been wearing since school speech day, so agonising on what to wear is kept to an absolute minimum.

Skirt length is a good indicator of what sort of woman you're dealing with in the office. Slightly above the knee is your normal executive, well above the knee is your predatory ball-breaker and well above the waist means adjustment is clearly required after hasty visit to the Ladies. Skirts just above the ankle denote elderly secretaries working in family engineering firm back offices with a tendency towards minor nervous ailments. Never say to a business-woman, "Oh it's that old dress again," especially if she's your boss and works in the fashion industry.

Women's jewellery has many meanings. Never trust a woman with more rings than fingers – no good ever comes of them. Similarly, beware women sporting a huge amount of jewellery all over their body. They are probably selling on commission and before you can say "Tupperware" you'll be sitting in their front room getting the hard sell on some delightful mother-of-pearl brooch and tiara combo.

Women live in abject fear of walking into a meeting and being confronted with another woman wearing exactly the same outfit. Fortunately men don't feel the same way otherwise in every meeting there would be at least one man storming out saying, "Oh my God, he's got exactly the same polo shirt and chinos. It's him or me."

Dressing down

Dress-Down Friday used to mean the carpeting you got from your boss at the end of the week for not having done any work in the rest of the week. Nowadays, Dress-Down Fridays are an incredibly generous gesture by companies that let you wear casual clothing on Fridays as long as you don't have a meeting or any meaningful work. Which means if you dress casually you're obviously not working hard enough.

Since the collapse of communism, Dress-Down Fridays have done more than anything else to impair the smooth running of capitalism. Business suits are for doing business in. If you're wearing a welder's helmet people expect rivets, if you're wearing a suit people expect business but if you're wearing shorts and sandals people expect you to be on your way to San Francisco with flowers in your hair.

Of course, when the managing director says you can dress down that doesn't mean you can come to work in a luminous thong. You have to wear smart-casual clothing. Smart-casual is a particular kind of attire not found anywhere outside the working environment. It's been specifically designed not to be smart or casual. It is in fact more of a uniform than a suit because if you're a man smart-casual can only mean polo shirt and chinos. If you're a woman it means anything under the sun except four-inch black stilettos.

In trendy companies that are permanently dressed down, the introduction of Dress-Down Friday would lead to the rapid establishment of a nudist colony. Instead they should have Dress-Up Fridays, where everyone has to come to work in a twelve-piece suit, spats and a monocle. This would also give them a valuable insight into what it's like working in a rural solicitor's office.

Handbags

A working woman's handbag is an office, washroom, databank, first aid centre, counselling department, long-term warehouse, travelling suitcase and financial department all rolled into one chic little off-the-shoulder number.

Women's handbags also have a separate mini handbag in them which is like a lunar module that goes out from the main mother handbag on smaller voyages. There is also a substantial business compartment in women's handbags which will generally hold the personal organiser, itself the size and weight of a full desk drawer. Small photocopiers have been known to fit comfortably in larger handbags.

There is a dark inner pocket in most handbags which harbours women's mystical personal things, connected with strange and hushed druidical rites that seem to come round on a monthly basis. However deeply these strange personal things are packed into the handbag they always pop out and land in the middle of the desk when the personal organiser is pulled out at the start of an important meeting.

Women are very conscious of bag snatching, especially when on foreign trips, and sensibly clasp their bags with both hands firmly against the body with the strap wound twice round their body and through their legs much like a parachute harness. Men should beware of touching or interfering with a woman's handbag in any way as this is tantamount to sexual harassment.

Every woman has something odd in her handbag that, should she suddenly be buried by an erupting volcano, would give archaeologists a thousand years from now cause for endless speculation and debate. These items include things such as Primus stoves, hacksaw blades, valances, hockey balls, red Y-fronts and petrol caps. Interestingly, when a woman's handbag is emptied completely, it dies.

Briefcases

In the commercial world it is the height of bad taste to have anything business-related in your briefcase. Briefcases are for taking the contents of the stationery cupboard home with you at the end of the day. Only photocopier repairman have their work in their briefcases – fifteen different screwdrivers, a copy of the *Sun* and a list of exotic, faraway locations from where the vital missing part will have to be shipped in a couple of months' time.

When it comes to briefcases, size is important and, amazingly, smaller is better. Really top executives have briefcases so slim that sandwiches will only fit in if they are evenly spread Marmite on thin-sliced white bread. A briefcase larger than A2 constitutes an art bag and you run the risk of being mistaken for an advertising account executive, which is the business equivalent of a personal hygiene problem.

Some briefcases have concertina sections which expand to hold pyjamas, computers and overhead projectors. Remember to clear this out when you come back from trips abroad otherwise you'll open your case up for a key presentation and your wife's nightie will billow out on to the boardroom table. Alternatively, don't take your wife's nightie on business trips.

Briefcases with combination locks can resist the most determined attempts to get into them, especially by the people who own them. When you're in airport arrivals being hassled by a Colombian customs officer, it's comforting to know that the likelihood of you getting your combination right under pressure is the same as winning the National Lottery two weeks running.

Business generally is more relaxed now and some people go to work with their papers in a satchel or knapsack. Be warned that some areas of business are less relaxed than others and if you're a top merchant banker you won't get very far if you roll up to meetings with your papers in a Buzz Lightyear lunch box.

Hairstyles

You can tell all you need to know about people in business by their hairstyle. With women the rule is big hair equals big business. With men it's the opposite. The less combing stuff you have on your head the more folding stuff you have in your wallet.

Everyone in business acknowledges that bald men are great businessmen, fantastically funny and highly sexual. Everyone in business has to do this, otherwise bald men would never have the confidence to come to work. Men with shaved heads are slightly different. They're either in design or they're fanatical members of the local gun club. Very occasionally they're both and you only find this out when you criticise their creative concept and get shot.

There is one person in every office who has had a transplant of hair from their armpit to their head. They do this to give them renewed confidence and it must work because how else would they have the guts to walk around with a hairstyle that looks like a gerbil has crash-landed on their head?

Women at work sometimes have what they call a bad hair day. To a man their hair looks no different, but to the woman concerned it feels like she's had five minutes under a muck spreader. When this happens, women will sometimes put their hair up. Don't take this opportunity to tell them they've got a dirty neck. Occasionally women will have a good hair day. You'll notice this because they keep flicking their hair round in a slow motion, shimmering arc. Men have a bad hair day twice a year. It's called a haircut.

Facial hair and business don't mix. Having an honest face is important in business and there's no such thing as an honest handlebar moustache. There are rare instances where men with beards succeed in business, but however well they do it's impossible to shake of the suspicion that somewhere deep in their wardrobe lurks a pair of sandals. There is also the added worry that somewhere in the beard there will be a piece of egg.

All types of facial hair need to be trimmed. You can't have a serious negotiation with someone who has what looks like the roots of a pot plant growing from their nose. Similarly, well-defined and arched eyebrows are good for expressing interest in what someone is saying, but they must be kept under control. If you can open a revolving door with your eyebrows, they're probably too long.

Shaving is a daily exercise for working men to prepare them for using a lot of soft soap and flannel at work, being on the razor's edge of competitiveness and not ending up with blood on the carpet. Having unsightly stubble is not an alternative unless you are hugely successful and don't give a damn or hugely unsuccessful and don't give a damn. Women approach their own stubble in the same way that farmers do – burning it, slashing at it, ploughing it back in and using all sorts of dangerous chemical defoliants. The only difference is that farmers plant winter barley afterwards and women don't.

12

EFFECTIVE COMMUNICATION

Communication

What separates us from the animals is our use of language. A shoal of a million fish might not be able to write *Romeo and Juliet* between them, but they can change direction as one in the blink of an eye. Using language, a human team leader can give an instruction to a team of six people and have it interpreted in six completely different ways. Language has made communication all but impossible for office workers.

There are two basic problems. Firstly, talking. Some people think before they talk. These people are so rare they often get mistaken for prophets or Messiahs. Some people think as they talk so they're not quite sure what they mean until they've said it. Some people just talk and are noise in search of a thought. You don't really listen to these people, you just have them on in the background, like daytime television. Some people think but don't talk but these are so few and far between that they are lumped in with the people who don't think or talk.

The talking problem is compounded by a second problem: listening. Generally, someone who gives the impression that they're listening is in fact just waiting politely for you to stop talking. While waiting, they're thinking about what they're going to say. Those who do listen do so only until what you've said sparks off a thought of their own, then you become background noise. Saying something to someone is like throwing a stick for a dog. As soon as you've thrown the stick they're off – they don't need the reason for you throwing it in the first place.

Some people make a big display of listening intently and cock their head alarmingly as they do so. However, they're usually listening for something to back up what they already think rather than listening to what you think. For instance, you can talk to an IT person for an hour about fishing and only get a response when you accidentally mention that you got a megabite. That's why most conversations in reality are two beautifully dovetailed monologues.

Effective listening is active, not passive. By leading people on, encouraging them to give more detail and generally giving every impression of getting the message, you can extract an enormous amount of information from a person without betraying a single thought yourself. Indeed, the talker will go away thinking you're an incredibly interesting and like-minded person.

Given the double whammy that people don't think before they speak and that people aren't listening anyway, it's not surprising that communication is our number one problem. When things go wrong in business it soon becomes clear that everyone thinks they did the right thing and the fault was actually in the communication. Of course, the wonderful thing about communication is that it's a no-man's-land for blame as everyone either meant the right thing or understood the right thing.

Mission statements

Mission statements are the business equivalent of writing a letter to Santa Claus. If you boiled down the mission statements of the top fifty companies, what you would have left is a lump of fat that read as follows: "We are committed to being world leaders in our industry. We will do this through delighting our customers by the world-class quality of our products and services. Our people are our greatest asset and we are committed to developing and training them. We respect the environment and are conscious of health and safety in everything we do."

What this means is: "We must make sure customers buy enough of our products to keep our shareholders happy. We will value our people as much as they are worth to us and comply with regulations concerning health, safety, environment etc."

If mission statements are really to inspire, they should read more along the lines of: "We are going to be a fantastic place to work for three reasons: firstly, we're all going to make shedloads of money because customers can't get enough of what we do; secondly, we're going to have an office environment that's just like home but without the children; thirdly, we're going to rip the arse out of the competition and leave them for dead."

Instead of missions, companies need concrete targets such as: we are going to market an electric car in four years; we're going to develop a legal mind-expanding drug in three; we're going to reinvent pensions in one. Unrealistic? Try the Kennedy mission statement: "We're going to put a man on the moon by the end of the decade."

Just imagine how the Ten Commandments would have sounded written like a mission statement: "We're committed to people living long lives and keeping their possessions. Parents will feel honoured and we will have a culture of openness and honesty in which everyone will love each other. Oxen will be respected etc." It all sounds fine and dandy and not something you'd have any issue with. However, when it comes to rock-solid commandments, it suddenly sounds a lot more challenging: "Thou shalt not kill; Thou shalt not steal; Honour thy father and mother."

That's why mission statements should take the form of commandments, so that everyone knows exactly where they stand. "Thou shalt meet thy targets; Thou shalt communicate internally at all times; Thou shalt take risks and think creatively; Thou shalt motivate and lead your team." And of course, if you didn't shape up, you'd go straight to hell. Mind you, if you're not doing these things already, your business is probably already going to hell. If this is the case, you can always cheer yourself up by reading your company mission statement.

Making telephone calls

An increasing amount of business these days is done over the phone. Or rather, it would be if anybody ever answered the phone. In fact there are certain individuals in marketing who have been playing continuous telephone tennis since the last century. Very often the original people who left the first message have moved on or are now dead and buried.

Generally, the reason calls don't get answered is because people are always "in meetings", which can mean anything from a critical management buy-out to picking their nose in the stationery cupboard. When the person you want is "in a meeting" you should always ask if it's an "internal meeting". If it is, this automatically implies that their meeting is an utter waste of time and money and should be immediately interrupted as you need to move the entire business forward.

Never have a greeting you can't do in one breath. So avoid something like, "Good morning, Smokehouse Industrial Strength Creativity, you're speaking to Angela Braithwaite, how may I direct your call?" By the time you've said all this, you'll sound like a heavy breather. A much better approach is to simply treat your caller as if you were married to them. When the phone rings, answer with, "Yes, darling?"

When you call a big company the first thing they will tell you is that your call is going to be recorded for your own protection. After they've done this and they finally put you through to a human, tell this person that you too are recording the call for training purposes. This will keep them on their toes or, alternatively, it will make them think you've never used the phone before and they will be very patient.

Top business people never hold. Only small unimportant people like customers hold. If someone says "Can I pop you on hold?" simply pop your phone back in its cradle and let the other person call you back. You can then pop them on hold while you make the tea or attend to some other critical business issue. Never wait in a queue. There isn't actually a queue. It's just you waiting for a machine ringing in a soundproof cupboard that's been forgotten about by everyone for years (or at least that's what it'll feel like).

Having said that, any amount of holding or waiting is better than having to leave a written message. Inevitably the person you speak to sounds as if they've just taken their head out of a bag of glue and you know that your message getting through is as likely as successful contact with aliens – especially after you've just finished spelling out everything in detail and they say, "Hold on, I better get a pen."

You should only make a conference call if the other parties are in Belgium, Swindon, Fallujah or other places you have no desire to see. Never accept a conference call from Barbados or the Seychelles. It's much more efficient and productive to go there yourself. Remember, with conference calls there are always three people in the other room who don't say anything and are busy making rude gestures every time you speak.

Phone manners are important and there's nothing more annoying than people who don't say goodbye and just hang up as if they're working in some sort of busy New York newsdesk. The trick with these oh-so-busy people is to phone them back immediately after they've hung up and say, "I think we were cut off. What was the last thing you said?" Then put the phone down.

Answering telephone calls

A nswering a phone in an office generally means speaking to a customer or your boss. As neither will call unless they want something, answering the phone will probably mean doing work. Rule Number One, therefore, is don't pick a phone up unless you know it's a social call. As you'll never know whether an incoming call is social or not, it's best to make a lot of pre-emptive outgoing social calls.

Managers always get terribly upset about unanswered calls and pretend that it could have been someone offering millions of pounds of new business. You know that's very unlikely because you've actually just had someone on the phone offering millions of pounds of new business and been so rude to him that he rang off. Managers try to improve telephone answering by instituting policies where you have to pick up any phone within five rings. Happily the policy doesn't say anything about slamming it back down immediately after picking it up.

Having more than one phone on your desk used to mean that you were enormously important. In fact the more your desk looked like the local telephone exchange the more important it meant you were. Not any more. Nowadays, if you're really important, a phone ringing on your desk is about as likely as a seagull landing on it.

Instead you have teams of people screening your calls and anyone with an axe to grind is immediately transferred to the customer careline where they are patronised to death.

Business is being revolutionised by direct-line services. This is where you phone in and speak to someone who sounds like a cheerful speak-your-weight machine. One of the reasons they're so cheerful is that they have computers in front of them which store all your personal information. All they need is your postcode and they can tell you your inside leg measurement and exactly how much you earn. You can then order an airline ticket, a jumper or even a mortgage, sure in the knowledge that if you're not happy with anything you can phone them up again and get an engaged signal for a week and a half.

There are a lot of security procedures on the phone which generally involve asking you personal questions. The favourite one is, "What is your mother's maiden name?" With the rise in the number of unmarried mothers this will have to change pretty soon, perhaps to something like, "Have you any idea who your father is?" If they start asking you questions such as, "Do you wear high-heeled shoes in bed?", they've probably gone beyond the security procedure to their own personal gratification procedure.

The most annoying part of ordering on the phone is that they repeat everything you say. When you've just told them that your name is Smith, they'll say, "That's Sierra Mike India Tango Hotel", as if they're speaking from Heathrow flight control. It's all you can do to stop yourself saying, "I can't hold her! The starboard engine's on fire!" Before these direct-line people finish, they always ask whether they can use your details "to provide information on other carefully selected services that might be of interest to you". The correct response here is, "Foxtrot Oscar."

Mobile phones

The marvellous thing about mobile phones is that wherever you are, whatever you are doing, you can keep them switched off so no one will bother you. If you do use them, you can make calls from virtually anywhere. For example, around about mid-morning you can call the office from underneath your duvet as long as your partner can make realistic motorway service-station noises.

There are two places where everybody automatically hates you if your mobile rings – restaurants and funerals. In both cases it's best to give the impression that the call is so vital that you absolutely had to answer it. Say something like, "Hello, Mum, is Dad out of intensive care?" Of course this doesn't work so well if you're actually at your father's funeral.

Blackberries and other less cool-sounding PDAs are very popular in business because they have solved the eternal problem of how to get on with important work when you're stuck in an utterly unimportant meeting. However, if it's your meeting you probably think it's very important, so arrange to have a text sent to everyone present which says, "Turn it off and pay attention."

In the old days you knew when your phone was ringing because you were on one side of your desk and your phone was on the other. These days when a mobile phone rings in a train, for example, sixty-five executives reach for their pocket/briefcase/handbag. The good news is that you can now download individual ringtones that only you will recognise. The bad news is that when your phone rings with the call of a mating sperm whale, a carriageful of people will think you're a complete idiot.

Of course, mobile phones are especially useful for anyone who spends a lot of time away from the office; most bosses, for example. Many business people use their phones in their cars. Of course this is strictly forbidden unless you have a hands-free set. Men tend to ignore this rule because they are used to driving virtually hands free while they excavate the inner recesses of their nostrils with one hand and fiddle with their genitals with the other.

Voicemail

Talking to yourself has always been a sure sign of madness. That's probably why you always feel slightly silly when you have to leave a message on someone's voicemail or answer machine. No surprise, then, that the favourite message left on the nation's answer machines is a single expletive followed by a crash as the phone is banged down.

The second most popular message is, "Got your message. Just returning your call." This returns the ball to their court and lets you stop playing with a clean conscience. The third favourite message is something like, "It's John, give me a call." This is generally left by people with such a unique and unusual name that they don't feel the need to leave a number or a message or any other useful information.

There are other people who don't so much leave a message as a life history. They ramble on and finally get to the point where they're telling you how they've improved their golf swing, when the time runs out and you don't get the vital message that your office is on fire.

Half the reason why people don't like leaving messages is because of the ridiculous greetings you have to listen to. Most common amongst these is, "I'm not here right now." It's patently obvious that they aren't there, but what makes it doubly annoying is the fact that they usually are there but just don't want to speak to you.

Not much better is, "I'm either away from my desk or on the phone." If they're going to give that level of unnecessary detail why not say, "I'm either standing just out of reach of the phone, in the loo or making love on the boardroom table. Please leave a message and I'll get back to you as soon as I've finished my post-coital cigarette." If this sort of thing annoys you, just leave a message along the lines of, "I'm not here either, so don't bother ringing back."

It's getting to the stage now when people who actually pick up the phone in person are forced to say something like, "I'm sorry, I am here at the moment, please speak to me now so I won't have to get back to you as soon as possible."

Email

Email was supposed to give us the paperless office but someone forgot to explain this to bosses who still arrange for their secretaries to print out all their messages and leave them in their in-tray. They then dictate a reply and get their secretary to send a reply on email just to show that they are coping with the white heat of technology. Remember, this is the same man who gave the "Our Future is Technology" speech at the annual conference.

Email buffs have little abbreviations such as IMHO which stands for "In My Humble Opinion". Sadly, these people don't seem to understand that no one in real life actually says "in my humble opinion", so it really doesn't need abbreviating. They also use little signs like :-) which, if you turn your computer on its side, looks like a smiley face. Emails from advertising creative departments are usually signed off *}§ – this means I am lying flat on my back, utterly stoned, with my stomach making strange gurgling noises.

Working in the post room is not generally a career choice for most people. Yet with the epidemic of email most people spend half their working lives slaving away in their own personal computer post room. If you're going to get more job satisfaction, you need to get out of the electronic post room and do something more interesting. Real communication happens in three dimensions. You need to see how people react to what you're saying and that means seeing their body language, their eye contact and them bursting into tears.

Many emails are biodegradable. If you let them sink to the bottom of the pile and go unanswered, they will eventually become irrelevant. To some people, doing this might seem like just about the most daring and suicidal thing you could possibly do in an office but if something really matters the person who sent it will eventually speak to you to ask you about it. And then real communication can begin, often in your industrial tribunal for gross negligence.

Some really annoying, petty people insist on asking for a receipt that their email has been received. These are the same people that complain they've got 500 emails in their mailbox, which is not surprising as they've generated two-thirds of them. Don't ask for receipts and don't send receipts. If it really matters that much that someone gets something, why not go and ask them?

Sitting at your computer is a lonely business and email is a way of pretending that you're actually in a social environment. You can also flirt or gossip online while pretending to work. Some people generate email in order that they will get more email in return. If you want to have a rich social life sitting at your computer by all means send lots of fun, chatty emails. If you want to have a rich social life in the real world, turn your computer off and click through to the real world.

Many people send emails in order to cover their hind

portion. Often seven or eight people will be copied in to an email to make sure every possible person who had any conceivable reason to be interested is informed. Remember that you are generally empowered to use reasonable authority in your job without getting lots of people's permission. And if you make really big mistakes then a few covering emails aren't going to help you.

There are certain golden rules with emails that save a lot of bother: try to reply as soon as you read an email otherwise you'll be reading it twice; always read what you've written before you send it; if in doubt, delete; never confuse the forward and reply buttons; only use Copy To All where every single person really needs to know; never forward anything you wouldn't pin up on your wall.

The fax

When you accidentally phone a fax it gives out a little screaming noise. This is the electronic equivalent of the inner scream everyone feels when they're interrupted by some idiot phoning them. Occasionally a fax will spew out pages of blank paper, like the fax equivalent of heavy breathing. This either means that someone has put their fax in upside-down, or it's a summary of all the valuable work your advertising agency has done that year.

Early faxes had silly flimsy paper much like army toilet paper. (In fact the contents were often alarmingly similar.) This paper curled itself tighter than a Bedouin's slipper, came out in one long strand and took half the office to hold it down before you could read it. This was soon replaced by the plain paper fax which gave you ordinary A4 paper that only cost seven or eight times the price.

Most faxes have URGENT written on the top which means that if you receive one you must take it immediately with the utmost urgency and place it quickly and urgently in the big pile with all the other urgent faxes. Faxes also have a little warning at the bottom saying "Only to be read by the addressee". This is a warning that should you even just take a little peek at the contents you will get a flying visit by the Armed Unit of the Serious Fraud Squad. If you're worried about confidentiality and other people reading it, make the second page of your fax a big bold message saying "Mind your own business".

Remember that a fax often has the name of who has sent it on the top. So if you're faxing in your CV to some top-level company it won't make much of an impression if you get your local pizza restaurant to fax it for you. Junk faxes are faxes that arrive during the night which advertise West End shows on the point of closure. The worst form of junk fax are those advertising cheap rates for fax paper because if it weren't for their junk faxes you wouldn't need to replace the paper every five minutes.

There are still people who send you a fax and then follow it up with a hard copy in the post. These are the same people who work something out on a calculator and then whip out an abacus to make doubly sure everything adds up. Fax back a copy of their hard copy to say you've got it and ask for an acknowledgement by post of their receipt of your fax.

Internal communications

A lot of companies talk earnestly about how important internal communications are. By internal communication they mean the process by which the bosses tell everyone what is happening followed by a feedback stage where everyone can tell the bosses what is really happening. There is sometimes a third phase when the bosses sack everybody involved in the feedback process.

Of course every company in the world has an unrivalled internal communication system. This is called gossip. It takes a multinational company five years and a lot of pointy-headed consultants trailing huge invoices to communicate a new vision to everyone in the company. But if the chairman were to be found cross-dressing in the stationery cupboard it would get round every cubicle in the company before you can say, "Let's keep this quiet, shall we?"

Gossip is a highly technical and complex form of communication. For example, messages are rigidly prioritised. Personal sexual revelations always take absolute priority over any business message. Of business gossip the most exciting is new people in new jobs. Of course the hottest news would combine the two, along the lines of, "Anita slept with every single candidate for the IT manager job, and they've all got second interviews next week."

The proof of good gossip is that the first reaction is, "No!!!" Good gossip can't wait and meetings have to be organised immediately for its sharing. It's estimated that half of all appraisals, data mergers and top-level strategic planning are simply a good old gossip. Email is great for gossip but will never really replace good old-fashioned face-to-face bitching. That's because it's almost impossible to imply or insinuate something when you have to type it and when there's also a chance that you might mistakenly send it to the person involved.

Conferences

Conferences are the business equivalent of going for a curry. Everyone thinks having a conference is a fantastic idea, but you always end up drinking too much, talking bollocks and feeling sick for days afterwards. One of the things that contributes to this queasiness is the themes used for conferences. Ninety per cent of conferences have the theme "Simply The Best" or "Playing To Win". If conference themes bore any relation to reality, at least one in three would be "We're Up Shit Creek".

The best conferences of all are sales conferences. This is where sales reps are called in from the country's motorway service stations and join together in a roller-coaster ride through the heights of passion and depths of emotion that go with the launch of a new brand of toilet cleaner. Many of these conferences require an overnight stay in the local hotel. This naturally leads to some frantic bedroom hopping by people who would be shocked and disgusted if they found their teenage children doing the same thing while they were away.

The biggest fear in the business world is having to make a speech at a conference. This is for several good reasons. The first good reason is that you generally have absolutely nothing of interest to say. The second equally good reason is that no one in the audience has the slightest interest in anything you have to say even if it was of any interest, which it isn't. For example, when you're the IT director, it's your job to make sure the IT works. If it does work they know already and if it doesn't, they don't want to hear your pathetic excuses.

Speakers vary in quality at conferences. There are some, generally from the IT department, who lose their audience somewhere in the phrase "Good morning, ladies and gentlemen". If you do happen to be awake during their speech, listen out for the phrase "but seriously". This will be your only indication that a joke has been attempted. The chief executive's speech is often a high point of the conference in that things tend to go rapidly downhill after they've finished. Chief executives generally talk about working smarter not harder, which is a phenomenal waste of time because everyone in the audience knows that if they could work smarter they certainly wouldn't be working where they are now.

Conference speeches

Prepare for a speech by producing an outline of what you want to say on a single sheet of paper. Then sketch out a conceptual framework to convey that message. Then throw the piece of paper away and write down every joke you've ever heard. Humour is a very useful way to help establish a rapport with the audience and what better way to announce a major programme of redundancies than with a string of dirty jokes.

A speech should last about the same time as a middle manager takes to make love. So about three bullet points should do it, followed by seven sides of closely typed apologies. Audio-visual support is a must in longer presentations. Really great speeches start with a joke, go straight into half an hour of completely gratuitous video clips of sporting moments, and then end with instructions of how to get to the bar.

Never speak from a lectern taller than you are otherwise you'll be remembered forever as the mysterious talking lectern. Also make sure you have a witty put-down for hecklers such as "You're fired". Speeches are written to be heard rather than read, so it's fine to use more colloquial phrases such as "Wake up, you bastards". Finally, the golden rule of speechmaking is tell your audience what you're going to say, say it, and then run off the stage to a waiting car.

If you're worried about large audiences, you can take comfort from the fact that you won't be able to see them because when you get on stage the lights will burn your retinas into the back of your head. The only area of the stage that has no light whatsoever is your notes, which are in complete darkness on the lectern. It's at about this time you realise you've left your reading glasses in your briefcase. Having prepared the speech for eight weeks, you now have to improvise a forty-minute speech based on the few words of your notes you can actually see.

Once you're up on stage you can then expect the technical faults to kick in. First your graphics won't work. If you're pushing a button, you'll accidentally push the wrong button and exit the programme altogether. If a professional's doing it for you, they will show the wrong graphic at the wrong time and skip over a couple just for the hell of it. If you're lucky, the lights will fail at this time only to come back on when you're tip-toeing off the stage with your arms flailing in front of you.

To be fair, the technical back-up may be immaculate. This allows you to mess up the presentation yourself. It's important to start well, which is why you inevitably choke on the first couple of words. When you can't say "Good morning, ladies and gentlemen" without provoking some kind of coughing spasm, it's unlikely you're going to dazzle and enthral for the full hour. Don't forget you can lose your voice at any time during a presentation. If you have a joke with a punchline this is normally when your voice says adios.

To fight nerves it's a good idea to grip the lectern with

both hands but not too tightly because they're only temporary structures and often collapse beneath you. The really brave can leave the lectern completely and walk around the stage pretending to be natural. Just be aware that you have in fact walked into complete darkness, your microphone is about to give you more feedback than a year's worth of appraisals and, at the furthest point away from your notes, you will forget your name, your job and everything you've ever wanted to say about anything.

Remember that the only thing keeping your audience from slipping into a permanent vegetative state is the prospect of coffee. It doesn't matter if you're the first speech of the day and you've only been talking for three minutes; no one is ever going to complain if you manage to choke out, "That's it from me, let's break for coffee."

13

MARKETING, SALES AND CONSULTANTS

Marketing

In marketing there is an unspoken rule which says, "If it ain't broke, fix it anyway." That's why one day you'll nip into the shops for your favourite product only to find it says, "Now with added mango." This can happen to any product from carpet slippers to disposable nappies.

Gone are the days when you could sell a simple product. You now have to sell it with bells, whistles and widgets, in a luminous, foil-wrapped, biodegradable, re-sealable, low-calorie, unleaded, easy-scoop, microwaveable, non-biological, galvanised, sustainable package with extra vitamins, fibre, minerals, anti-oxidants and nutritious gravy, with a lifetime, no-quibble, fully comprehensive, interest-free, fire-and-theft, sale-or-return, three-for-the-price-of-two, buy-now pay-later guarantee, now with added mango.

Naturally, people are now hankering for the good old days when you could pop down to the grocer and buy a straightforward hogshead of butter, a cubit of flour and a quatrain of sugar, sure in the knowledge that the only additives would be a selection of insects, worms and microbiological nasties. In those good old days you didn't need tamper-proof tops either, because you knew if you got anywhere near anything worth tampering with, you'd get a thick ear.

When they're not adding something, marketing people

are claiming better performance – often for their products. Toilet paper has been getting "even softer" for about thirty years and, unless it started as slabs of granite, it must be reaching the limits of softness. At some point the marketing people will go into reverse and start claiming that each new roll is harder, firmer and more aggressive and they'll subtly change the advertising from a small puppy to a spiky-looking armadillo.

There are two types of customers: those who buy your products and those who don't yet buy your products because they haven't been exposed to your powerful marketing. There are all sorts of ways you can segment your customer base. A useful distinction is between those that have money and those that don't. You can then divide them into those who have brains and those who don't. Then sell your products to the ones with money and no brains.

Focus groups are very useful for understanding your customers. This is where you get a select group of customers together and, over some nice wine and nibbles, you ask them some probing questions about your products. You don't learn anything from these groups other than there is a small segment of your customers who, for a glass of wine and bowl of cheesy Wotsits, will turn up and talk bollocks about anything.

To be successful in the marketplace every product of service needs a Unique Sales Proposition, or USP. This is the thing that separates your product from all the other similar products out there and gives you competitive advantage. Only seven or eight companies are allowed to have the same USP at any given time. (Don't confuse USP with UPS otherwise you'll spend your entire marketing budget delivering parcels.)

One way of protecting your USP is to have a very strong and recognisable brand. This comprises a logo and a name which are both instantly recognisable. All the good ones have already been taken so if you haven't already got one you're likely to end up with the name Pathetica and a logo featuring a happy guinea pig. Once you've got your brand, make sure it appears everywhere in your company. A branded carpet in reception is a confident step towards a permanent place in the FTSE-500.

They say that half the money you spend on advertising is wasted. The bit that's wasted is normally the money you spend on the creative work. The other half is spent on long lunches and "brainstorming workshops" in country hotels with golf courses attached and is clearly money well spent. An advertising creative's job is to convert the last trendy film they saw into an ad for your toilet cleaner. The client's job is then to remove the trendy film out of their ad concept and replace it with toilet cleaner.

A famous marketer, who sadly died suddenly, once said "Innovate or Die". This is as true today as it always has been despite everyone innovating like mad in the interim. The way to innovate is to try new things and take big risks. This of course is almost always disastrous in the long term. The trick is to apply for a new job in the short term while your big new idea is getting maximum PR and the waves of laughter and derision from the focus groups aren't yet audible.

258

Corporate hospitality

Someone said there is no such thing as a free lunch. Whoever that person was, he clearly didn't work in marketing. The idea of a free lunch is in fact so powerful that a whole industry has grown up around it. This industry is called corporate hospitality and it's based on the fact that people who wouldn't dream of meeting you for an ordinary meeting will happily meet you for lunch, especially if it's served in a director's box before a rugby international.

Corporate hospitality is mostly done by suppliers for their clients and the idea is to get them so drunk that the years of appalling, overpriced service are wiped from their memory. Or, if they are not yet your client, to get them so drunk that they sign up to years of appalling, overpriced service.

No act of corporate hospitality is complete without everyone getting a big golfing umbrella with a logo printed on it. These are very useful at outdoor events because God clearly disapproves of corporate hospitality and tends to rain on it. Marketing directors in big companies can quickly tell how big their budgets are by the number of supplier umbrellas clogging up their hall at home.

There is of course a subtle line where corporate hospitality becomes downright bribery. This line is so subtle that most people from marketing never notice it, especially when they've just finished their second bottle of champagne and they've started mooning to the crowd from a box at Anfield. Naturally, finance departments rigorously disapprove of all freebies as for them giving out a biro with the company name on is tantamount to grand larceny.

In the end it's all about style. Do clients give their business to suppliers who fly them to Paris for the races or to suppliers who are working so hard on their behalf that their corporate entertainment amounts to no more than a couple of luncheon vouchers stapled to their invoice? Clients with their heads screwed on will go to Paris with the first company and give their business to the second.

Exhibitions

Drawing attention to yourself is not generally encouraged in business except in marketing, where acts of gross exhibitionism are highly valued. Nowhere is this more the case than in exhibitions or trade shows where hundreds of like-minded companies gather to expose themselves to the public.

The most difficult thing in an exhibition is working out how to display all the marvellous things your company does in a space the size of a teenager's bedroom. Unlike a teenager's bedroom, you then have to do everything in your power to encourage people to come in and spend as much time there as possible. It's also worth remembering that ninety per cent of people walking round exhibitions are your direct competitors who will be exhibiting all your great ideas, slightly repackaged, next year.

Free coffee and doughnuts will get people flocking to your stand even if you're exhibiting nasal hair conditioner. In fact just the word FREE is enough to get most people excited. Another good way of getting people interested is to do a live demonstration. This is all well and good if you're selling food processors or shoe-shine kits, but not so good if you're selling vasectomy shears or cremation services. The one thing that puts people off coming to your stand is big friendly marketing people

smiling everywhere. It's much better to have them standing to one side smiling intensely at the stand as if there
was something exciting happening on it.

Businesses should avoid having one sad person quietly
knitting next to a pile of dog-eared leaflets. The only interest you're likely to get is from still-life photographers and
fellow knitting enthusiasts. Also, remember that free
boiled sweets are not in themselves sufficient to influence
purchasing behaviour unless you're in the confectionery
business. What you need is a buzzy, happening atmosphere and this can be achieved by hiring actors to simulate intense interest in your stand. Make sure you
audition carefully because you don't want a troupe of
ham actors swooning with pleasure over your brochure or
weeping with gratitude when someone hands them a
business card.

The business card is the exhibition equivalent of
money: you've got it, the exhibitors want it. They'll be
offering all sorts of free prize draws to the Caribbean if
you'll just drop your card in their big glass bowl. Don't do
it. Once they've got it you will receive mailings twice a
week and be contacted continuously from here to eternity
by every sales person in the company, because possession
of your card means you are officially a hot lead. The secret
is to behave as if you were going to a casino and take only
the number of business cards you are willing to lose. Three
is a good number because, let's face it, it's very unlikely
that there are going to be more than three great new products or services you absolutely must know about.

When viewing the exhibition, the trick is to walk down

the exact middle of each aisle at a slow but even pace, glancing quickly at each stand before you get to it and then saying "No thank you" every five yards. This will ensure you escape the unwanted attention of all the exhibitors desperate to get hold of you and your card. If an exhibitor steps into your path and actually thrusts their card at you, don't panic. This actually gives you a spare card which you can then pop into the next glass bowl to give them another nice hot lead.

Research

If you're ever stopped in the street by a smart middle-aged lady with a clipboard who asks you intimate questions, you are either participating in market research or being propositioned by an astonishingly inept streetwalker.

Hiring a research company is for corporate chickens. It's like asking a friend to ask a girl if she fancies you. If he's really your friend he's not going to come rushing back with, "She thinks you're repulsive and you make her sick." Even if you have the world's worst product, don't be surprised when your highly paid research agency comes rushing back with, "It's a winner, let's go with it."

There are three sorts of market research: quantitative, where you ask how many people do things; qualitative, where you ask why people do things; and manipulative, where you just make things up. Take for example a disastrous West End show: quantitative research would say that ninety-seven per cent of people hated it; qualitative research would tell you that people hated it because it was "the theatrical equivalent of colonic irrigation"; manipulative research would tell you that the show was "Unmissable – fight to get a ticket!"

Not all research takes place on the street. Consumer labs are where you get a group of like-minded people in a cosy room with sofas and then you pay to sit behind a two-way mirror and watch them perform. If these research groups lasted thirty seconds people would just say, "Yeah, that deodorant smells good, I'd put it in my armpit." Instead they last three hours during which deodorant gradually becomes a metaphor for post-modern introspection or a beacon of hope for humanity. People say many things in research but one thing always remains unsaid and that is, "Of course I wouldn't spend any of my money on that."

Middle-aged ladies with clipboards have the opposite effect of a truth drug. They remind you of your mother so you instinctively lie to please her and stay out of trouble. That's why you shouldn't be surprised when consumers seem to have changed their mind shortly after you've spent millions launching a new product they said they loved. Remember, research has never been done on whether research works. Or, if it has, they're keeping very quiet about the results.

PR

PR companies make their money by following a simple formula. They scare the pants of major companies by talking about some X factor that could ruin their business and then charge a hefty retainer for making sure the X factor never happens. When it doesn't happen they claim a major victory and send you a series of celebratory invoices.

A very small part of what PR does is to help create awareness of your product. This they do by spending a fraction of their colossal retainer hiring a bunch of tired and emotional actors to hand out hastily prepared leaflets at your local station.

When choosing a PR agency remember that they work on the basis of the other form of PR, ie proportional representation. If they are representing a major oil company with a multi-million-pound account, your little piece of business will be given to a student placement to do when they've finished making the coffee. A good rule of thumb is that you should never hire a PR agency that is better known than your own company, because if you do, that position certainly won't change.

At the vile, slimy end of PR is the publicist whose job is to keep your face in the media. This explains what became of the boy at school who made it his mission in life to keep flushing your head down the lavatory.

Keeping your face constantly in the media is the psychological equivalent of his juvenile behaviour.

PR agencies are like advertising agencies in that they involve an almost continuous round of parties, lunches and general swanning about. The small but noticeable difference is that with an advertising agency you might have something to show for it at the end.

Sales

Saying you're in sales at a party is like announcing a death. But saying you're going to the sales is quite all right. That's because in this country selling is rather dirty but shopping is rather sexy. But then in this country we've always confused what's dirty with what's sexy.

All sales people have targets. Mostly the targets are confused elderly people who can be persuaded that it's normal to have four pension schemes all at once. Naturally, when someone says they're in sales you feel immediate contractions in your wallet. That's why sales people often pretend they're actually something slightly more socially acceptable, like a fur farmer or TV licence detector van operative.

At the bottom of the sales tree are double-glazing sales-men. You'll recognise them on the phone because they're just doing some research, they're not trying to sell anything and they just happen to be in your area. When they ask you if you're the homeowner, tell them you're just in to install the double glazing.

In sales you get the hard sell and the soft sell. The hard sell is where you get your foot in the door and shout through the gap until the homeowner calls the police. You then try and sell to the police down at the station. Soft selling means that people are more likely to buy from you if you get really pally with them. Funnily enough, sales people never get to like you so much that they don't have the heart to sell you an investment scheme that halves in value two minutes after signature.

Consultants

A consultant is someone in business with an ego so large it takes more than one company to support it. At a personal level, consultants work either by trying to inspire fear or trying to be friends. Trying to be friends with you is when they inspire the most fear.

Management consultants are much like medical consultants in that they're paid to keep a straight face while examining the shrivelled private parts of industry. Consultants often start with what they call a scoping exercise. This derives from the medical practice of getting you to drop your trousers and cough. The real point is to see how heavily your wallet hits the floor and to gauge how much can be removed from it later. The headquarters of big consultancy firms reek of expense. Just sitting in their reception has the same effect on your budget as cold water has on your gonads.

The acid test of a consultant is whether they can say, "Everything's fine, we'll be off then." No real consultant can. Instead they'll sell you a project that costs just enough to keep your profits suppressed to a level that requires further remedial consultancy.

All consultants claim to have worked with one successful company so they can say, "At BA we looked very seriously at matrix management." What they don't tell you is that they worked for BA as a student pulling chewing gum off seats in economy and the closest they got to matrix management was playing Connect 4 in the works canteen.

To be fair, consultants do leave you with a nice report. This lists all the figures your company has ever produced, highlighting enough mistakes for your financial director to keep very quiet when it comes to paying the bill. Somewhere at the back of the report is a summary of recommended actions. The first one, in heavily disguised language, says, "Make more money or you'll be neck-deep in cack." The other, in clearer language, says, "What you really need is another scoping study."

Agencies

Agency people are a lot better-looking than you are but this doesn't necessarily mean that they have more brains than you. Actually, they're probably better-looking and smarter than you are, which is why they're driving a Porsche and you're on public transport. However, the Achilles heel of glamorous agency types is that deep in their hearts they know they don't have a real job. When they've come up with some ludicrous piece of creative work, simply say, "That's lovely, but it won't work in the real world."

Agency people are divided into two types. The ones with good teeth and fast cars are known as account people. They have been specifically trained to talk rubbish to you without you noticing. If you think you're lucky enough to have an agency person who talks a surprising amount of sense, this is only because they've been exceptionally well trained. The other types are creatives. You're not allowed to see creatives because they're just too creative to interact with normal people. There's also the fact that they can only communicate in grunts and whistles.

When you schedule a meeting with your agency, always allow them to be an hour late. This gives them time to decide what shade of black to wear. Clients should always wear suits even if they don't normally wear them for their daily job. Suits are what people in the real world with real jobs wear. If you insist on wearing your casual wear, remember that agency people are on the cutting edge of metrosexual fashion and will always make you look as if you dress exclusively from Poundstretcher.

Always volunteer to reserve your agency parking spots for their overpowered, brightly coloured motors which in effect you pay to keep on the road. Make sure this is the spot in the car park that is under the branches of a large tree. Then fill the overhanging branches with many different types of birdfeeders to attract a large number of hungry and incontinent birds. In this way their car can have the same experience as you will in the meeting with them.

There are so many agencies out there, you might find it baffling choosing one. You can actually pick an agency at random because they all offer inspired creativity, incredible insight into your business and a unique collaborative approach. Behind their receptions, agencies are pretty much all the same. The only thing to beware of is the agency that seems to have too many sofas. If they're for the creatives to relax in, they're obviously not doing enough work. But if the sofas are for you to sit in, then you should expect a very long wait for any sign of productive output.

Agencies are like lovers. At first you think they're sex-on-toast but after a while you notice they have a number of unpleasant and expensive habits. The best way to get rid of an agency is to ask them to re-pitch for the business along with two younger, slicker and smaller sex-on-toast agencies. You can then tell your old agency that they lost in a fair fight (unless of course they come up with the best work).

14

MAKING THINGS HAPPEN

Strategy

There are only four types of strategy in business: acquisition, divestment, sales growth and cost cutting. In order to pick which one to use, simply see what the previous chief executive did and then do the opposite. Alternatively, you can choose by timing. All strategies last for seven years, so simply see what the company was doing fourteen years ago and repeat.

Strategies are only for the benefit of City analysts who on the whole don't really understand business. In fact it's fair to say that what people do in the City and what people do in business are two completely different things. Strategies are big headlines that analysts understand. If your strategy is bold enough then your share price will go up. Good CEOs will have a really bold strategy and then immediately cash in their share options.

Strategies, like share options, generally peter out somewhere in the higher reaches of middle management. A greater proportion of people who attempt to climb Everest actually reach the top than strategies successfully reach the bottom.

Possibly the most powerful and successful strategy is to do something called running the business effectively. This involves getting great products quickly to customers, at a reasonable price with good service. Sadly, much of business education is dedicated to finding complex reasons for ignoring this strategy. It takes a really great leader to admit that it's very simple to run a business.

Initiatives

To get ahead in business you need to be the sort of person who is seen to be doing things. Of course, everyone is doing something, namely their job. Therefore, people who do something over and above their normal jobs are noticed and get promoted. That's why thrusting executives need to get themselves well and truly associated with an initiative.

An initiative is born when it gets a name. Your job doesn't have a name, therefore it is not an initiative. But invent something called New Horizons or Vision 2010 or Raising Our Trousers and you have an initiative. There are only six types of initiatives: quality, cost control, empowerment, innovation, team working, and customer service. These come around as perennially as the grass and once you've been through a whole cycle it's probably best to leave the company before your cynicism becomes a threat to the entire organisation.

You don't have to be creative to have an initiative – that's what consultancies are for. They are experts in creating the biggest possible deal out of the smallest possible idea and finishing up with the largest possible invoice. They have drawers full of original ideas tailor-made for your company. All initiatives must include the following: a ring binder of worksheets which are jargon-free, interactive and fit neatly on the top shelf; a printed mousemat to show just how easy it all is to understand; and a launch conference where everybody interacts and understands during the day and drinks and forgets during the night.

Once you've got your initiative it's very important to talk about it in a special way so that everybody knows it's not just normal work you're wasting your time on. Initiatives are never a revolution, but always evolution, or the other way round. And of course an initiative is never just an initiative because it's going to become "our way of working"; it's also going to require "the involvement of everyone" and "change will come from the top" unless it's "bottom up"; the initiative will then involve "a step change in performance" and put us up where we belong which is "industry leaders", "best in class" or "simply the best".

All initiatives have a life cycle: bold idea, expensive execution, painful rollout, brief excitement, apathy, decay, loathing, death. Once you have championed an initiative, employed eye-wateringly expensive consultants and the fancy colour printing has been done, it's absolutely vital that you take maximum credit as quickly as possible and then get the hell out and give the whole project to some other poor booby to implement. This person will then take the blame, bitterness and anger that naturally arise whenever anyone tries to change anything.

In any large organisation there are lots of initiatives going on at any one time. Therefore your own personal initiative could be to blow the whistle on any one of these ongoing initiatives as being a pointless waste of time and money. Everyone will rapidly agree with you and you will get all sorts of bonus points for being so tough and rigorous and single-minded. Of course, the most radical and productive initiative would be one called "The Year of Getting on with our Jobs without any Ridiculous Initiatives". But you won't get promoted for suggesting that one, so best to keep quiet. Or maybe you could suggest a little "Back to Basics" initiative.

The right person

Getting things done in business, as in life, is simply a matter of making sure you speak to the right person. Sadly, the right person doesn't normally exist and ninety per cent of the time you have to make do with the ignorant, lackadaisical half-wit who has the intelligence and initiative of a hub cap and who single-handedly seems to be causing a slowdown in the economy.

Somewhere in a mythical land far, far away is a person who knows exactly what you're talking about, has your information at their fingertips, can do exactly what you require, can do it immediately and seems to take a genuine pleasure in serving you. If you ever, by some miracle, come across such a person, you tend to be so pathetically grateful that you actually forget why it was you called and instead start thinking about finding out who they are and marrying them.

Occasionally you get so cheesed off with the customer service assistant you're speaking to you attempt to escape them by asking to speak to their supervisor. Remember that the supervisor has been trained to use the phrases "I can appreciate", "let me take your details", and "we're making every effort" in any combination they see fit in order to pacify you. Never, ever get angry with supervisors. Apart from the fact that it won't get you anywhere, you should remember that you only have to deal with the half-wit on this one occasion, whereas the bonus of the supervisor depends on his/her performance day in day out.

Everyone in the office is the right person for something. Everyone in their own way has either the experience, the programme, the form, the docket, the knowledge or the key to make something happen in the easiest manner possible. But then the next immutable law in business is that when anybody wants to do this particular thing the last person in the universe they will ask is you. Had they but asked you, everything could have been done and dusted in seconds. But they didn't and so they have to reinvent the wheel, take their driving test and do a couple of crash tests while you're standing patiently at the finishing line. In this way everyone has to learn to do everything from scratch. That's what they mean when they talk about a learning organisation.

Networking

The old school tie used to be the fan belt of British manufacturing industry, which explains why we no longer have one. However, in business they still say it's not what you know, it's who you know, which is a bit depressing when you've just completed fifteen years of formal education.

Some people will swear that the secret of business success is something called networking. Funnily enough, they'll be telling you this in the corner of the local library where they've been sitting reading the recruitment ads in *The Lady* for the last few years. Networking is named after the old Network South-East train service: it's a waste of time and money and there's no guarantee it'll get you anywhere.

You'll know someone is networking because they'll give you their card within the first thirty seconds of a conversation. After about two minutes of telling you how brilliant they are, ask them whether they would like your card. As they couldn't give a monkey's about anybody else's card, why not return their own card to them and watch them slip it straight back in their pocket.

At parties, really keen networkers talk about "working a room". You'll know who they are because, while everyone else in the room is enjoying themselves, they'll be the ones working like stink. Their aim is to ask everyone in the room what they do and dump them after three seconds if they're not useful. To networkers the person over your shoulder is always more interesting than you are. Overall, this creates exactly the same impression as if they'd walked round the room handing out cards saying "Don't ever do business with me".

Getting organised

Every so often at work you decide things have got to change. Anything can trigger this feeling: suddenly realising you've been in a temporary job for five years; finding an urgent memo addressed to you by someone who has left the company; or the growing awareness that your job description reads like a rehabilitation programme for the criminally insane.

Once you're gripped by this feeling, you very rapidly decide that enough is enough. Those of a violent disposition would at this stage go out and destroy a bus stop. The rest of us start doing a number of things that we wouldn't normally do. The first thing you do is clear the decks for immediate action by slicing the end off your rubber, untangling your telephone cord and putting ninety per cent of your paperwork in the bin.

You then clear up your computer by reorganising all your files into an easy-to-use, logical system that divides everything into three folders: Work, General and Other. For the first time since you joined the company you decide to empty the wastebasket on your computer and free up two-thirds of the memory. You get into this so much that you accidentally throw away all your major applications and can't work for a week.

Having completely cleared your computer you then

tackle your in-tray. You work incredibly hard for three hours without even looking up and do a month's work including all the really nasty things that you've been putting off like customer service. After that you phone people in the office you don't like and say no to their stupid time-wasting ideas. When you've got that off your chest you then make a neat list of all the things you're going to do to really get you into the fast lane of life, like learning German, getting an MBA and cutting back on the ice cream. Finally, you decide that this sort of efficiency means it's high time you had a new high-powered job, so you register with an executive placement agency.

By this time your burst of energy is beginning to fade and you move into the smug and content phase where you admire your empty desk, your clean rubber and your empty in-tray. This phase very rapidly becomes the extended lunching and shopping wind-down period, where you handsomely reward yourself for being so good.

Once you finally get back in the office, you spend what's left of the afternoon telling everyone how hard you've worked and catching up with your social calls, interrupted only by the executive placement agency calling you back to offer you the superb job opportunity of the person two promotions beneath you. At the end of the day you go home still smug enough to justify the following four weeks of complete idleness at work.

Meetings

Half of every working day is spent in meetings, half of which are not worth having, and of those that are, half the time is wasted. Which means that nearly one third of business life is spent in small rooms with people you don't like, doing things that don't matter. The only reason people have so many meetings is that they're the one time you can get away from your work, your phone and your customers.

People say that the secret of a good meeting is preparation. But if people really prepared for meetings, the first thing they would realise is that most are completely unnecessary. In fact a tightly run meeting is one of the most frightening things in office life. These are meetings before which you have to prepare, in which you have to work and after which you have to take actions. Fortunately, these meetings are as rare as a sense of gay abandon in the finance department.

Time in meetings is always different from real time. A quick ten-minute catch-up can fill a whole morning. One of the reasons for this is that work in meetings doesn't actually start until someone says, "I've got a meeting to go to." A cancelled meeting is the sweetest thing in office life. One way of making your life in the office a lot easier is to book a lot of unnecessary meetings and then cancel ninety per cent of them. This leaves your diary almost completely free for relaxation, or work if you're that way inclined.

When you go on a week's holiday you miss on average ten meetings, but curiously no one misses you. That's because meetings have a life of their own, regardless of the people in them. The moral of this is that whenever someone asks you to be in a meeting say that although nothing would give you more pleasure, sadly you are going to be on holiday. The following week, carry a suitcase rather than a briefcase round the office in case someone spots you walking past a meeting you are supposed to be in.

Meetings are a lot like heaters in old taxis – they just recycle hot air until you get a headache and have to open the window. Airtime in meetings is generally hogged by those with the loudest voices and the biggest egos. Normally these are the very same people who come up with the worst ideas. All the best thoughts and ideas in any meeting are had by the people who contribute absolutely nothing and sit in total silence. Most meetings are spent either talking about problems arising from work that hasn't been done or talking about work that needs to be done to tackle problems. There are so many of these meetings that there is very little time to do any work or solve problems, which means only one thing – more meetings.

Breakfast meeting are different from other meetings in that people are asleep at the start rather than at the end. One of the problems with business breakfasts is that you can never eat what you normally have for breakfast. No one's going to be impressed at a top-level breakfast meeting if you're tucking into a bowlful of Coco Pops. Instead, you have to eat things that only religious zealots and French people would touch, like grapefruit and croissants.

Latecomers

In every corporate statement of values there is something about respecting other people's time. Similarly, in every organisation there are people who respect other people's time so much they insist on using as much of it as possible. The worst offenders are people who always arrive late for meetings.

Many men in business measure their masculinity in terms of how late they can be for a meeting. For them, arriving on time would show you were extremely junior or that you had so much free time you could afford to sit around waiting for other people to show up. Being late to a meeting shows everybody in it just how little time you've got and how lucky they are to have someone so in demand at their meeting. This largely explains why a meeting that starts on time is as rare as understatement in the marketing department.

There is a finely graded scale of lateness for a meeting. Anything between five and ten minutes doesn't really count because that time is taken up pouring the coffee and swapping notes on how bad the traffic is. Twenty minutes late is the entry level for serious latecomers, with half an hour to really impress. Anything over half an hour risks people not waiting.

Behaviour on arrival demonstrates where latecomers

are in the office hierarchy. Lower orders will shuffle in timidly and then sit there like a lemon understanding absolutely nothing because they missed the crucial bit about why everyone's there. Other boss-like people will breeze in and start pontificating about a subject that has actually been covered in the first ten minutes (anything that has been agreed before they arrive will need to be unagreed on principle in order that their input is recognised as vital in the decision-making process).

Latecomers always shake their head in a bewildered way and let out a great sigh as though their lateness was the result of some cosmic conspiracy against them rather than the fatness of their head. Strangely, were there to be a meeting at which promotions were being given out on a first-come, first-served basis, those very same people would be at the front of the queue.

It's very difficult to combat this kind of perpetual lateness among bosses because it stems from a form of intoxication, generally with the sound of their own voices. The only solution is not to invite them to the meeting in the first place. Sadly, this isn't normally possible as most meetings are actually called by bosses to lecture everyone on teamwork and mutual respect. Try referring to a perpetually late person as, for example, The Late Mr Duffy. This can be pretty disconcerting after a while, especially if you use it in all internal memos.

Doodles

Doodles are the tattoos of the office world through which people inadvertently express their innermost thoughts and desires. The most common doodle in the office is pretty flowers which means you are dreaming of all the nice things that are happening outside your meeting. Then there are heavily shaded arrows which mean get me out of this meeting now. Finally there is a man with an axe buried in his head. This means that the meeting should have ended an hour ago.

Doodles tend to have a life of their own. What starts as a light shading of a capital letter can become, by the end of a three-hour meeting, something that looks like a fresco from the Sistine Chapel. Sometimes doodles become so complex and elaborate that they are mistaken for the real output of the meeting. For example, the design of the new Scottish Parliament was actually some vigorous cross-hatching by someone bored rigid in an early planning meeting.

A little bit of doodling is expected in a meeting but don't overdo it. The person running the meeting won't thank you if you keep asking them to pass coloured markers so you can shade in your masterpiece. Doodling means people are bored so if it's you who's doing the presentation and everyone is doodling, you should finish soon. If they start asking for more paper, finish immediately.

Report writing

Reports are the office equivalent of cones in the road. They're not actually work themselves but they're a big, clear sign that real work might be done at some stage. In the meantime they slow everything down and cause anger and annoyance all round. Researchers (who do nothing but write reports) have done a very interesting report that suggests that the ratio of report to work is normally about ten to one in the average office.

The quickest and easiest way to write a report is to change the names in the last report you wrote. When you do this be aware that there will always be one name that escapes changing and that will be in the sentence, "We are committed to personal service to ...." The other thing people always forget to change in reports are the headers and footers, which you only notice are completely wrong in the taxi on the way to your presentation.

Reports always start with background which no one ever reads so you might as well talk about what you did in your summer holidays. If you want something to be noticed in a report, call it an executive summary; if you don't, call it detailed non-executive background. Big salary rises for yourself should go in footnotes to appendices unless you're dealing with lawyers, who always check the fine print. For them, put the hidden stuff into the "ethical policy" section of the document where it will pass entirely unread.

There's nothing worse than preparing a huge report for someone who flicks straight to the costs on the back page and then sits with their nostrils curled while you slog through the previous eighty pages of pre-rationalisation. To combat this, have the costs and conclusions on a separate piece of paper. You can give them this at the end of the presentation or, if they like what they've heard, go back to the office, double the costs and send them on later. Or you can be radical and start with the costs, do your long presentation and hope they've recovered from the shock by the end.

Most reports could be written in one line: "This is what we should do, this is why, this is what it will cost." However this doesn't reflect the five weeks' work you're supposed to have done on it. You therefore need to pad it out in the time-honoured fashion by increasing the type size, doubling the spacing and putting in huge appendices of meaningless figures. Another way of quickly thickening a report is to turn it from a brief Word document into a thick PowerPoint presentation. Remember that colour printing increases the business value of any document by more than thirty per cent.

Bosses never read or write reports but they're forever asking you to write one. The reason for this is that they don't really know how to manage you. What they're hoping is that somewhere in the report they'll find a clue of what to ask you to do next. More often than not the time it takes you to write the report gives them time to

GUY BROWNING

think about something else for you to do which, of course,
has absolutely nothing to do with the contents of the
report. Reports are also a handy tool for which bosses take
the credit if they're good and blame you if they're bad.
That's why the cover sheet with the author's names is
always the page that gets changed the most on any report.

Process cheese

Given the fact that most people are working incredibly hard, it's amazing how little gets done. That's because however hard you work, there are always powerful forces working equally hard against you. Chief among these is something called process cheese. This is a combination of bureaucracy, stupidity and inertia and forms the main strata of every company in much the same way that mozzarella forms the main strata of most pizzas. Trying to change something in the office is like trying to cut a clean piece of pizza; it's impossible without pulling a whole load of stringy process cheese with you.

Process cheese is why you can't do something as simple as moving your pot plant without consulting widely, communicating internally, briefing your team, scoping the project, hiring consultants, preparing a budget and making sure everything is consistent with health, safety and environmental regulations, the company's mission statement and EU directives regarding transportation of agricultural products.

The second reason it's difficult to change anything is because everyone is scared stiff of the risk involved. To them, risk can mean failure leading directly on to written warnings, sacking, unemployment, eviction, marital breakdown, family break-up, impotence, alcoholism, madness, drug addiction and death. So when you suggest a minor improvement in the stationery ordering system, don't be surprised that people see you as a bringer of destruction and death.

If you actually manage to get something done, don't relax and get all complacent. In business it is a cast-iron rule that whatever you are empowered to do, your boss is empowered to undo. It also follows that the longer it takes you to do something the quicker your boss can undo it. If you're doing a project that represents your life's work, it's therefore a good idea to make sure you're not reliant on the sign-off of someone who suffers from intermittent post-lunch tetchiness.

The biggest impediment to change at work is something called the committee stage. This is like the Wells Fargo stage in that it generally gets ambushed by hostile forces with completely different agendas. Committees gather people together who know nothing about a subject, allow a five-minute briefing on a three-year project, and then expect to generate an intelligent response when most minds in the room are focused on how heavy the demand is going to be for the pink wafers on the biscuit plate.

Generally, if you want something done you should do it yourself. However, if you really want to get something done in the office, don't do it yourself. Get your boss to think they've done it themself and make sure they get all the credit for your hard work. That appealing prospect explains why many people never attempt anything in the first place.

Mistakes

Most companies these days encourage you to be creative and take risks. They then encourage you to find alternative employment when you make a series of monstrous blunders in your search to be different and edgy.

Some companies are so successful in encouraging their employees to make mistakes that they have gone out of business before you can say "empowerment". Of course, the trick is to learn from your mistakes and you may hear business leaders using the phrase "a learning organisation". This is a business that makes so many mistakes that the whole company is a kind of University of Disaster.

Remember that everyone in business makes mistakes, except for your boss who would never have done anything so stupid. Naturally the more mistakes you make, the more experience you have. That's why job advertisements always require two years' experience. This ensures that you've made all your mistakes at the expense of another company and you'll now be relatively harmless.

For every success in business there is an equal and opposite failure. At the office dinner you can bet you'll be sitting between the equal and opposite failures. Some mistakes are so colossal that no one can ever admit to them. For example, you'd be hard pushed getting an

American to admit what a disastrous mistake their War of Independence was.

Changing anything in business is a victory in itself and, if the change is big enough and you are quick enough, you can often claim the credit for a great success before the magnitude of the disaster becomes apparent. Hence the prevalence of early retirement in the IT industry.

Filing

The most popular letters for filing under are G for General, R for Rubbish and F for Forget. Being filed is a permanent vegetative state for documents from which they are rarely, if ever, brought back to life. However, if you were ever to throw away a document, it would inevitably be required the next day for a major business presentation.

The ancient Egyptians used to bury their dead surrounded with things that might be useful in the afterlife. Modern office workers surround themselves with filed documents that might be useful at some later stage, but never are. Had the Pharaohs chosen to bury themselves in filing cabinets instead of giant pyramids they would have remained completely undisturbed for ever.

Filing cabinets are all booby trapped so that when you open more than one drawer the whole thing collapses on top of you. More sophisticated filing systems have special fancy locks that don't allow you to open more than one drawer at once. Naturally everyone assumes they must have lost the key to the drawer they can't open and immediately give up. There may be another reason you can't get a filing cabinet drawer open and that's because all those little tab things stick their heads up at the crucial moment and get wedged under the drawer above.

If you feel the urge to throw the whole filing cabinet out of the window, do so. Companies that lose all their files in a big fire generally have a fantastic period of growth, innovation and excitement for months afterwards because everyone can forget everything they did in the past.

Deadlines

Deadlines in business are like wedding anniversaries: missing one is easy but dealing with the thermonuclear fallout that follows is less easy. Most office deadlines are purely imaginary. Your boss will whip you into a frenzy to get a report done in a day because it's an absolute deadline and then, when you've made a fearsome hash of it, they'll give you another two weeks to rewrite it.

Every deadline in business translates directly into a deeply etched line on the face. That's why lawyers and bankers are always so smooth-cheeked and why all journalists have faces that look like road maps of downtown Warsaw.

Deadlines used to be things that you could gaze at from a safe distance. Nowadays, if you're not working to a crushing deadline you are, in all probability, dead or a plumber or both. In general, the tightness of a deadline is a direct reflection of the incompetence of the person who gives it to you. "Time is tight on this one" means "I've only just thought about this because it's happening tomorrow".

The odd thing about deadlines is that at some stage you will have agreed that the time you've been given is perfectly reasonable. To avoid this, always say "That's totally impossible" even if you've just been given a month to write a one-pager on something. Negotiate an extra month in which you can do the work, leaving one month completely clear for more recreational work activities.

Deadlines and panic always walk hand in hand: the closer the deadline, the more the panic and the greater the cock-up. Simple tasks take four times as long with deadline pressure due to panic-induced blunders such as manufacturing the wrong bit or boarding the wrong long-haul flight. The trick with deadlines is to save time by panicking as soon as you get them.

Working late

Anyone who finds themselves working late on a regular basis is on a steep downward spiral on a coconut mat marked "stress". Sadly, it's their own fault because when they were asked in their interview if they were prepared to work long, unsociable hours, they didn't reply, "No, I prefer to work short, sociable ones, thank you."

Of course, definitions of what late working means vary. If you work nine to five and you find yourself still in the building at 5.35 then that's a pretty late night. If, on the other hand, you run your own business and you leave the office before last orders then that amounts to a half-day.

In big offices the definition of late working is if you know the names of the cleaner's children and the name of the security guard's unfortunate skin condition. You also know you're working too late too often if the first time your children are old enough to stay up late enough to welcome you home is shortly before they leave for college.

Nevertheless, working late does have its advantages. Obviously the first one is that you can get more work done in three hours than you can in three normal working days because you're not continually distracted by the personal phone calls you're making all the time during the day. It also gives you a golden opportunity to rifle through other people's personal papers and generally get yourself up to speed on the office dirt. Generally it's while you're casually flicking through the managing director's in-tray that you discover the one other person who habitually works late happens to be the managing director.

You know you're working late when you start to feel sorry for yourself; you know you're working really late when you order a pizza in for your supper; you know you're working incredibly late when you dig the pizza box out of the bin and eat the one cold slice you couldn't eat five hours earlier.

THE FUTURE

When we look at the future of the office, one thing is absolutely crystal clear. But no one knows what that one thing is, so we'll just have to blunder on as usual.

However, there are some predictions we can make with complete confidence. The first is that there will be more and better ways of communicating, all of which we will continue to ignore, and instead we'll keep people in the dark until something goes disastrously wrong.

The other thing that will happen is that offices will become more like home and home will become more like the office. Offices will get incredibly cosy with trendy cafés, soft furnishings, casual clothing, crèches and sympathetic lighting, while an increasing part of the home is taken up with computers, printers, filing and desks. Eventually people will be desperate to get to work, where they can drop off their kids, sink into some soft furnishings, get some decent food and generally kick back and relax.

Bosses will disappear. When everyone's working from home, no one's going to want a boss in the spare room. Everyone will be their own boss. Bosses will become good communicators so we'll all have bosses that listen to us rather than the other way round. The downside of this is that we'll have to think of something worth saying.

The big question is, will people still have desks? If you have a palm device that computes, communicates and does absolutely everything electronically, desks will need to be completely redesigned. They will have coffee cup holders and Chocolate HobNob dispensers; a buttock rest for passing gossipers; a pop-up video display of your loved ones (updatable); a range of drawers designed to hold a banana, yoghurt and copy of *Heat* magazine; and a single sheet of A4 paper and a pen in a glass case that you can break in an emergency.

The even bigger question is, will we, in thirty years' time, still be struggling to work on unreliable, over-crowded trains, working in teeming, peeling offices for rude and unpleasant bosses, doing repetitive and largely useless work? Given the state of our pensions, the answer is yes, we probably will.